A Tapestry of Grace

Also by Edward K. Ziegler:
    A Book of Worship for Village Churches
    Country Altars
    Worship in the Christian Home
    Rural People at Worship
    Welcome, Little Stranger
    Brethren Win Men to Christ
    Rural Preaching
    The Village Pastor: His Work and Training for
        Tomorrow's World
    Simple Living
    Tell Us About the Church of the Brethren
    One Hungry Beggar

A Tapestry of Grace

Edward K. Ziegler

The Brethren Press, Elgin, Illinois

Cover design by Ken Stanley

Library of Congress Cataloging in Publication Data

Ziegler, Edward Krusen, 1903-
    A tapestry of grace.

    Includes index.
    1. Ziegler, Edward Krusen, 1903-   2. Church
of the Brethren—Clergy—Biography.   3.   Clergy—
United States—Biography.   I.   Title.
BX7843.Z53A35   286'.5   [B]   79-25331
ISBN 0-87178-834-9

Published by The Brethren Press, Elgin, Illinois 60120

To the two daughters of God
who have so richly shared my life:
Ilda Bittinger Ziegler
and
Mary Vivolo Ziegler;

And to all my brothers and sisters
who share in the grandeur and misery
of the Christian ministry

TABLE OF CONTENTS

FOREWORD

I am honored by Edward K. Ziegler in being asked to write a foreword for his book. It tells the intriguing story of his long, diversified, wide-ranging, exciting and service-filled life, which up to this point
has covered three-fourths of the twentieth century. It sweeps across the
world from state to state and leaps with ease to other countries and con-
tinents. His life also involved a whole spectrum of related Christian services: preaching and pastoring, teaching at various levels from elementary
to college and seminary, widely varied administrative duties, including
service on the national staff of the Church of the Brethren, membership
on the denomination's General Board, moderatorships, including being
national moderator of his denomination, lecturing, the writing of many
books and articles, editing magazines, particularly a quarter century as
editor of *Brethren Life and Thought*. Through all of these changes the
thing to which he always returned, as if to the heart of his calling from
God, is preaching: preaching and all of the pastoring and nurturing responsibilities which go with it.

I feel somewhat qualified to write about Ed for I have known him
rather intimately through all of the years and experiences of the book except for the very earliest. He came to West Virginia from Pennsylvania
with my sister, Ilda, after they met as students together in the Academy
at Elizabethtown. He became my brother-in-law in the earlier part of this
century and after nearly fifty years, when my sister died, he became and
continues to be my deeply loved and highly respected "brother."

This book reveals throughout what I was able to observe in a lifetime
of experiences close to him. He is a person of highly diversified capabili-
ties and gifts. He grew through the years as he nurtured and expanded
these gifts. He has become one of the Church of the Brethren's gentle,
committed patriarchs still serving the denomination with distinction.

One instance will illustrate this growing, maturing process. When
Edward and Ilda entered their first pastorate in the hills of West Virginia
after their marriage, they faced some new expectations and situations
which this book describes. The mountain people were especially familiar
with two different types of preaching from the itinerant or occasional
preachers who came through. Some liked the one kind better, some the
other. One was loud, explosive, "hell fire" preaching. The sinners on the
back seat were going to hell, and soon! Some of these preachers could not

easily find the line between God's condemnation of the sin and God's love for the sinner which led Christ to die for him. The other type preacher was gentler. The sin was not less evil but the sinner himself was clearly and always for loving and for redemption. Edward had a good voice, a good physical presence. He could be the "hell fire" preacher or the loving preacher; he could "scare" or he could lead. Those of us from the West Virginia hills who knew the gentler side of the mountain people and sang their sad and catching ballads with them hoped he would develop along the gentler and leading way. He did, though as he records, it took some time in Virginia, and a Paul Bowman and others, to help him feel his true calling.

This growing Edward K. Ziegler developed a kind of leadership and preaching which enabled him to be a gentle moderator, a good missionary, a kind and loving husband and father, a denominational and an interchurch leader through all of the accumulating years. His growing has never stopped. This book tells that pleasant story.

Desmond W. Bittinger

PREFACE

I am deeply indebted to many persons, far more than I can name, for their help and counsel in writing this story of my pilgrimage, and urging me to undertake it. But special thanks to Barbara Smith, who typed hundreds of pages, deciphering my scrawling longhand script; to my careful editor and friend, Fred W. Swartz; to my long-time friend and brother in love, Desmond W. Bittinger, who read more than one version of the manuscript, and has written a gracious foreword for the book. But most of all, I am indebted to my wife, Mary Grace, who has encouraged me to write, surrounded me with the serenity and home comfort needed to get the job done, and finally, typed the final script. To her, and to all others who have helped and encouraged, Thank you!

Edward K. Ziegler
Frederick, Maryland
Summer, 1979

INTRODUCTION

Today I am seventy-five years old. My life pilgrimage has been long, rich, crowded, exciting. I have been a farmer, a teacher, a pastor, a rural missionary, a college and seminary professor, a denominational bureaucrat, a church moderator, a traveller, an author, an editor, a photographer, a family man. I have lived in eight states and in India. Too much a rolling stone, perhaps? Indeed there have been disadvantages in never living more than six years in any one place since I was seventeen years old, and in working at many kinds of tasks. But this "on the road" kind of life has had compensations, too. It has given me a rich kaleidoscope of experiences, and has thrown me in the company of a host of different persons who have moulded, guided, educated and blessed me by their friendship and trust, and their sharing of the treasure of life with me.

For some years now family members and friends have urged me to share my experiences of life and ministry and what I have learned through them all, so that others who are younger in ministry of any kind might profit from my pilgrimage journal. Up to now I have not taken these urgings very seriously. I doubted whether such a book would be useful, even if it could be published. But not long ago a wise and dear friend said to me, "God has given me a message for you: 'You must not die until you have written the story of your life.'" I could not laugh that off! Now that I have lived far beyond the biblical threescore years and ten, and have been an ordained minister of the Gospel for more than fifty-six years, I think it time to take this plea seriously.

My real purpose in writing is to be of some help to young persons who are entering a ministry, whether ordained or lay. I want to share as best I can the grandeur and the misery of ministry, the struggles and joys which have been the tapestry of grace in one man's ministry. A poignant statement by the Apostle Paul in Ephesians 3:7-8, could appropriately be my text in beginning my story:

> Of this Gospel I was made a minister according to the gift of God's grace which was given me by the working of his power. To me, though I am the least of all the saints, this grace was given, to preach the unsearchable riches of Christ and to make all men see. . . .

It seems to me that through all the varied experiences of living and serving in the ministry which I have had, God has been at work weaving a tapestry of grace, far beyond my counting and deserving.

So here the story begins. I will try to tell just enough of the story of my life to show how the rich stuff of heritage and culture have been handed down to me, and how I have tried to pass it on to others through the ministries entrusted to me. I am not a self-made man. Many persons have moulded, influenced and taught me. I know that I am different from every other person, often painfully, embarrassingly different. I have loved deeply and totally, and I have been greatly loved, far more than I have deserved. So the story of my life is not so much a record of achievements as it is a colorful tapestry of human relationships. My story can only be meaningful as it is filled with the stories of persons around me — my family, my teachers, my students, the people of my parishes, my colleagues in ministry, my enemies (I am thankful they seem to be few), writers whose words have kindled thought and flame in my mind, lovely and loving persons with whom I have been bound in the strong ties of family. In all of these persons, I have seen so much of God!

This pilgrimage has been a faith journey. Years ago I read with mounting excitement and sometimes with shocked dismay series of articles in *The Christian Century* on "How My Mind Has Changed." Well, this story will be a succession of such revelations, too. My religious faith has not been a static or frozen faith. There have been low and high points in it, sometimes corroding doubts, often visions and insights that have sustained me and lighted my path.

I can honestly describe myself as a churchman. The Church of the Brethren nurtured me and my family through the generations, and this church called me to ministry, trained, sustained and commissioned me. Almost every kind of ministry within this community of faith has at some time been entrusted to me. Now as an "elder" in the church I have time to reflect, to see visions and dream dreams for my church. Perhaps the length and breadth of this ministry, the wisdom of the leaders of the past who taught and befriended me, the wide acquaintance with the total church which I have acquired across the years may entitle me to speak my concerns and proclaim my hopes and dreams for the church I so deeply love. This may be a small but helpful distillation from the story of my pilgrimage thus far.

I have many regrets. My education for ministry was acquired piecemeal, and in it I took too many shortcuts in preparation. Always some new and challenging task seemed to beckon, and I would postpone the needed year or more of rigorous training. I rejoice that my younger colleagues in ministry are for the most part avoiding this pitfall and are coming to their ministry far better prepared than I was.

As I look back on the years of ministry, I regret that most of my pastorates were too short, that I yielded too promptly to the lure of greener pastures somewhere else rather than working patiently through the things which needed doing where I was.

Some of the things I hoped to do I have not achieved. And while I can see many ways in which God clearly guided me into places and tasks where I can honestly feel good about my achievements, I also clearly see the areas of failure and defeat. My clay feet often stumbled!

Sometimes a tongue too ready to express judgment and criticism, to sound off without knowing all I could know, or without hearing the other person or walking in his shoes, have caused me to make tragic mistakes and to wound and alienate other persons. I am now well aware of the shallows in my life and thought. I know that I have sometimes thought myself indispensable. Consequently I was away from home too much and did not give my wife and children as much of myself as they needed and deserved.

I wonder if the shallows I now see in my life-long ministry make me like the legendary North Platte River, said to be an inch deep and a mile wide at the mouth! Perhaps my readers, and certainly God, can judge better than I.

CHAPTER 1

Train Up
a Child

I was born on January 3, 1903, in the big farmhouse on my grandfather's farm, two miles from Royersford, Montgomery County, Pennsylvania. My parents, Harry Horning and Mary Hunsberger Ziegler lived in half of Grandfather Jesse Conner Ziegler's house. My father was the farmer, for my grandfather was spending most of his time working for the church and raising funds for Elizabethtown College.

My father and mother were married on December 21, 1901, a week after my father's twenty-first birthday. My mother, Mary Hunsberger, grew into her early teens in the home of her parents, Abraham and Hannah Hunsberger, near Creamery, a mile from the Skippack Mennonite Church, of which they were life-long faithful members. She went to the county seat town, Norristown, to live with and work for her aunt, Mary Detwiler, and here she began to attend the little Church of the Brethren on Barbados Street. At eighteen, she was baptized into the church by the pastor, William Howe.

My earliest memories in my childhood are of my grandfather Hunsberger taking me on his knee to teach me the German alphabet. When I was four years old he died of cancer. Grandmother lived alone for a few years, then lived most of the time with us until my parents moved to Maryland after I left home in 1924. Grandmother was kind but funny, often impatient with us children. When she was angry at us she would mutter German epithets at us, but would often treat us to hard candy or cookies.

When I was four years old, Grandfather Ziegler was again taking an active part in the farming, and my Uncle Howard was grown enough to

16

do much of the work. So my father rented a farm, the Pennypacker place, two miles away near Trappe. We lived there only a year, but my little sisters and I found it a fascinating place to explore. We were right beside the "Pike," the main road between Philadelphia and Reading. By this time automobiles were occasionally seen on it. When we heard one coming my sister Esther and I would run from wherever we were playing and sit on the front steps to watch it chug by.

About this time I thought I was too big to play with my dolls, the well-worn stuffed clown and Foxy Grandpa. One morning Mother built a hot fire under the caldron to boil apple butter; I threw my aged and grimy dolls into the fire. I was ready for more manly toys!

Esther was seventeen months younger than I, a sweet tempered beautiful child. We never quarreled. But Florence, as soon as she could follow me around, was different. She had a hot temper, and could screech like a scorched wildcat. So I teased her just to hear her scream. Often she did provoking little things just to annoy her big brother. Mother was always quiet and gentle, but our antics sometimes exasperated her to the point that she would threaten to spank us with the mush paddle. I was the older, so usually it was I who bore the blame. Once when the sound and fury were too much for mother to endure, she tethered me to the big pear tree in the back yard by a ten-foot length of clothesline. Then my little sister prowled just out of my reach hissing and taunting me! Now, seventy years later, we have long been the best of friends.

After one year on the rented farm my father bought a fifty-two acre farm near Limerick, two miles west of our former home. We named this place Green Valley Farm. The farm house of white-plastered field stone was nearly two hundred years old. It was surrounded by tall old walnut trees. It had a big sunny living room and kitchen combined, with deep window seats where mother's geraniums thrived and where we children loved to sit to read or play games. The farm buildings, a big red barn and henhouses, corn cribs, woodsheds, and an ice house, stood on the hillside. Below the house a small stream named Lodle Creek flowed across the farm. Along its banks were stately old willow and walnut trees, and dense thickets where blackberries hung like purple jewels in late summer. Here, too, were many varieties of wild flowers, and birds nested in great abundance. In the long meadows beside the creek our cows spent the lazy summer days.

We lived twelve good years on this lovely farm. We were poor, but we never knew want. We grew most of our own food. During most of our farm years my father would go to Norristown every Friday with a wagon load of farm products to sell to a select group of customers who depended upon him all summer for fresh, tasty vegetables, apples, eggs, butter, poultry, and home-cured meats.

In the cool cave-like cellar under the house there was a small cold spring. The pure water flowed through a rock-hewn trough, where large cans of sweet cream waited for the Thursday churning into golden butter. Hundreds of glass jars of vegetables and fruit stood in the cellar for winter use. Thursday was a very busy day. In addition to churning a hundred or more pounds of butter, chickens were killed and dressed, baskets of vegetables washed and packed, and in the cooler months a fat hog or two was butchered, to be cut up and processed into sausages, pudding, scrapple, spare ribs, chops, and roasts. Hams and slabs of bacon were soaked in brine, then smoked slowly until they were a rich aromatic brown. Mother made crocks of delicious cottage cheese, rubbery cup cheese, and sometimes rows of highly pungent and aromatic balls of Dutch cheese to sell.

Whenever there were school holidays I went with Father to market. Hitching two of our farm horses to the covered market wagon, we would be on our way before five o'clock in the morning for the twelve mile drive to town. There we would go from house to house selling all the good things. I do not know how much profit was made from this business, but I know Father took quiet pride in having the best butter, meat, and vegetables, and that the fifty or sixty families who bought from him fully trusted him and waited eagerly for his Friday appearance.

Our farming was varied and intensive. Father was a good steward of the soil. He was most careful to till the fields so that no gullies formed. Though he used some commercial fertilizers, he knew much about organic farming and growing green crops to plow under. We did our farming without benefit of tractors and never had electricity or milking machines. We worked hard and put in long days; up at five in the morning to milk a dozen or more cows and feed and care for all the stock before a hearty seven o'clock breakfast. Then from April to November we would be out in the fields and orchards plowing, planting, cultivating, and harvesting. Again in the evening we did the chores of feeding and milking, gathering the eggs, running the cream separator and seeing that all the animals were securely bedded down for the night. From these years on the farm, learning to care for the animals and sharing the many tasks, I developed a deep and lasting concern for our environment and the joy of cooperating with God in sustaining the good earth.

The long winter evenings were a special delight. After supper was over a small basket of apples and pears was placed on the round living room table. Father was a great reader, and he would settle down with the Bible, the Farm Journal, a book, or the texts of a correspondance course he was working on, all the while working his way through five or six big apples. My sisters and I usually had some homework to do. Mother sewed, mended and read. Often we would gather around the parlor organ to sing hymns.

Religion and the church were important to our family. Father and Mother were active members of the Mingo Church of the Brethren. There were two meeting houses: Mingo, just two miles from our home, and Skippack, six miles to the east. As far back as I can remember, Father was superintendent of the Sunday School at Mingo, taught the adult Bible class and served as church clerk. He took pride in keeping concise and accurate records of the quarterly church council meetings. Though it was still the custom in many churches for men and boys to sit on one side of the meeting house, women and girls and babies on the other, my parents sat together and kept us with them. We never debated whether we should go to church or not; it was a delight and as natural as our meal times. As soon as Sunday breakfast was over and everyone was dressed up, Father hitched one or two horses to the two-seated carriage and we were off to church.

As the children grew—there were seven of us altogether—the carriage became too crowded. By the time I was twelve, I usually walked. A short cut led down the dirt road by my grandfather's farm, then across a hill through some woods to the church. I think I learned to know every bird's nest, every wild flower, every wild strawberry plant and cherry tree along the route.

When I was young, Grandmother Ziegler had a dozen or so of the little folk in her Sunday School class. She taught us to sing, told us Bible stories and had a big chart with fascinating colored pictures. We sat on a long wooden bench, our feet swinging six inches from the floor, beside the big basement furnace. Later classes left little impression upon me until my early teens when Uncle Howard taught a dozen of the growing boys in his class in the "Amen Corner" of the church.

Between the Sunday School and the worship hour, when the weather was fair, everyone would visit a while out under the big maples and oaks. Time to worship was signalled by Peter Smith or Sam Hess, younger ministers, who would start singing a well-known hymn from the 1901 black hymnal. Boys from ten years up sat on the back bench, sometimes not too attentive. After a hymn or two the ministers took their places on a low platform behind a long table. Grandfather, as elder-in charge, was first in the line. Then came the other elders and preachers in order of seniority—Uncle Abe Grater, Uncle Levi Ziegler, Uncle Jake Conner, Peter Smith, Joe Cassel, and Sam Hess. Earlier, Great Grandfather Ziegler sometimes sat there, but he rarely preached, and only in German.

At this point in the service one of the deacons, standing in front of the table, would read a chapter from the big pulpit Bible. For years we read successive chapters from the Old Testament. Then all knelt for the long prayer, the ministers facing their table, and others turning and kneeling where they had been sitting. At the end of the fervent prayer, often in dignified and solemn language and led by one of the ministers, another minister wold pray the Lord's Prayer and all would rise. Another hymn was sung and we settled down for the sermon. Our ministers preached in turn, usually giving an exposition of the chapter which had been read. A few of the sermons were inspiring and full of homely admonition. Some were boring and showed little evidence of study. Uncle Jake Conner almost always preached short sermons based on a Psalm and always talked about the Creation and God's care for us. Grandfather's sermons were always thoughtful and earnest.

After the sermon another minister would rise and offer a few additional thoughts, "bearing testimony" to the sermon but rarely with new insights. Then he would call us all to kneel again for a prayer. After this prayer another hymn was sung. Then Grandfather would make a few announcements and say quietly, "You are now dismissed; go in peace." There would be a time of leisurely visiting, invitations to go along home for dinner were given and accepted, and we went home.

A special treat in our meeting for worship was the frequent visits of young ministers who were studying nearby at Ursinus College. A vivid memory is of a lovely Sunday morning in May when the apple trees in the orchard across the road were in full blossom. Through the open windows behind the ministers' table we could hear orioles and bluebirds singing, while Ralph Schlosser, a radiant, eloquent student minister preached a stirring and joyous sermon.

Every year the congregation was stirred and sometimes really renewed by a two-week "series of meetings" by a visiting evangelist. Each evening's meeting began with spirited singing of hymns; then would come a sermon which was either an earnest biblical exposition or a stirring call to follow Jesus and become a Christian. A few of the ministers would paint lurid pictures of the flames of hell or the glories of heaven. This was the time when young people "made their decision" and came forward at the invitation of the minister to publicly confess Christ. The success of these meetings was measured by the number of boys and girls and sometimes neighbors and their families who made public profession of faith and sought baptism into the church.

Just before my tenth birthday I responded to such an invitation one night when "Cousin Will" Conner from Virginia was the preacher. I was the only person who came forward at that time. Grandfather said that we would wait until warm weather for my baptism, rather than break the ice to baptise me in January. Cousin Will Conner was an artist with chalk who drew fascinating pictures before the sermon, preached earnest and serious sermons, and attracted large crowds. In his later years he became obsessed with the pre-millenial interpretation of eschatology. When we lived in Shamokin he preached two weeks in our church solely on the second coming of Christ. He became quite intolerant of other interpretations and was more and more gloomy and disputatious.

What did this decision mean to me as a ten-year-old? Simply, I think, that because of all my early home training and my belief that I was now old enough to make my own important choices, I decided that now I would follow Jesus and become a member of the church. I was not scared or coerced into this decision. I cannot recall having any fear of hell; I was attracted to the idea of following Christ. The night when I went forward, Father and I were the only ones from our family at the meeting. As we drove homeward, he talked very seriously to me about this decision. He was glad, he said, that I had done it. But such a decision meant that there would be some changes in my life. I would need to be kinder to my sisters, and even to the farm animals. I would need to be more truthful and must be careful to keep away from bad company and bad habits. He explained that faith in Jesus and becoming his disciple were a matter of behavior, not only going through the motions of being baptized and joining the church. This conversation was typical of my father's relationship to me. On another occasion he and I were returning from an evening at the church on a cold, clear, winter night. We drove along without speaking for a time. He was looking up at the sky, and began quoting softly, "When I consider the heavens, the moon and the stars which thou hast made, what is man. . . .?"

Grandfather Jesse Ziegler baptized me on Saturday, June 13, 1913, in the quiet little brook in the meadow below his home. It was Love Feast Day, and the baptism took place between the services. I was the first of his grandchildren to be ready for baptism and the last person he ever baptized. A few months later he was stricken with a crippling disease that lingered until his death five years later.

Love Feast was a highlight in our church life. A week before the appointed day, many members gathered to clean the church. The wooden floors were scrubbed and polished, the benches cleaned, the dishes for the supper washed, the tubs and towels for feetwashing were all scrubbed and made ready. A few days later, the wives of deacons and ministers met, often at Grandmother's home, to bake the communion bread. They made this a real spiritual event. Dough was carefully mixed and kneaded, rolled into a quarter-inch thickness, marked into strips an inch wide, and pricked by a five-tine fork to represent the five wounds in the body of Jesus. Then it was carefully baked and stored for the communion.

On Saturday afternoon the entire congregation gathered for the "Examination Service." Usually a number of visiting ministers and lay people came from neighboring congregations. The singing was especially hearty and satisfying. There would be two sermons. The first of a general nature, the second and main one directed at the members' need to examine their living for any unforgiven sin or any break in the fellowship of the church. A long prayer of penitence and a closing devotional hymn closed this service.

In the intermission, often members of the church who had misunderstandings or who were angry at each other met and worked out reconciliation, lest they be unworthy to commune. While farmers hurried home to feed and milk, deacons and their wives prepared for the feast. The benches in our meeting house were so constructed that every third one would be converted into a table by reversing the back. The bench in front of this one had a reversible back; thus with a minimum of rearrangement the entire meeting room soon was prepared for members to surround the long tables. Snowy white cloths were spread and a plate, spoon and fork, and a cup for water were set at each place. Early in the day the deacons had cooked large chunks of fine quality beef which was sliced and put on plates, two or three to each table. The beef broth was poured over broken pieces of white bread in large bowls. This tasty soup was placed so that each group of four persons could dip their spoons in the bowl. A tub of warm water, a large towel which had tapes to tie around the waist, a small basin of water and a hand towel were placed at the end of each table for the feetwashing service.

The communion bread, now broken into strips ten or twelve inches long, was placed on two platters on the ministers' table where the officiating elder would be seated. Here also were two pewter communion cups and a pitcher of dark sweet grape juice carefully prepared and saved by one of the deacons.

When the hour for the service came, the ministers moved gravely to their places behind their long table, with the officiating elder, usually a visitor, at the head. Then, the women and baptized girls surrounded the tables on one side of the house, the men and boys on the other side. When all were seated, and visitors who were not church members seated on side benches on the men's side, the service began. A hymn or two were sung. Then one of the ministers read the "feetwashing scripture," John 13:1-17. Removing their coats, the men began the feetwashing, and the women followed suit on their side. The person at the end of each bench tied on the large towel, sometimes at the very point where the minister read, "and Jesus took a towel and girded himself." Kneeling, he gently washed the feet of the neighbor on the right. After a fervent embrace and kiss and a "God bless you!", the one whose feet had been washed in turn washed the feet of the next person until all communicants had shared in the rite. Hymns were sung from memory during the rite, and a minister occasionally would rise and comment on the meaning of what we were doing.

After the feetwashing a prayer of blessing on the meal was offered by a deacon or minister. Then we enjoyed the delicious bread and beef and dipped up spoonfuls of the soup from the large bowls. I do not know why, but it seemed there was never such tasty meat and soup as that served at Love Feast. The meal was eaten in solemn silence and was followed by another prayer giving thanks for the meal. Two features of the service which are rarely observed today followed the supper. As a symbol of the deep sense of brotherhood, the "kiss of charity" was passed around the entire congregation, the elder initiating it by giving the right hand of fellowship to the first sister at the nearest table. After this rite, there was the reading of the story of the woman who broke the alabaster box of ointment and anointed Jesus, Matthew 26:6-13. It was explained that this was read because of Jesus' injunction that her loving deed should be remembered wherever the Gospel would be preached.

In preparation for the communion a hymn such as "O Sacred Head Now Wounded," or "When I Survey the Wondrous Cross" was sung, and the entire nineteenth chapter of John was read. The officiating elder then uncovered the trays of bread. All communicants stood for the prayer of consecration which he offered. When all were seated again, the elder broke off a small piece of bread and gave it to his neighbor saying, "Beloved brother, this bread which we break is the communion of the body of Christ." He in turn took the strip of bread and broke bread to his neighbor, with the same words. Another minister or deacon followed with a tray to replenish the strips of bread as they were exhausted. In the meantime the elder broke bread to each sister at the tables. Women did not at that time break bread to each other. When asked why, the elders would explain that since women had no part in the crucifixion of Christ they should not engage in the symbolic act of breaking his body! When all had been served bread, the elder would ask, "Has anyone been omitted in the breaking of bread?" I often wondered—what about the many people who were not a part of the church? Weren't they omitted? Then we would solemnly and thoughtfully eat the morsel of bread.

Much the same procedure was followed in passing the cup of grape juice. The elder would announce as he gave the cup of grape juice to his neighbor, "Beloved brother, this cup of the New Testament which we bless is the communion of the blood of Christ." As the common cup was passed, one for the brothers and one for the sisters, each would murmur the sacred words. For some reason we usually sang hymns while the cup was passed. The little children with their mothers at the tables were often given a morsel of the communion bread, but the cup was never offered to them.

The evening after my baptism I sat at the table with my father. The sense of solemnity and reverence was overwhelming. Though I am sure we younger members, and perhaps many of the older ones, had little idea of the profound meanings of the service, we had a deep sense of the numinous, of feeling that we were fulfilling the commands of Jesus, and a great sense of brotherhood. Somehow the congregation seemed more closely knit together, more sure and comfortable in our discipleship when we celebrated our Love Feasts.

Usually all the visitors were invited to our homes to stay overnight, and the church was filled to overflowing for the preaching service the next morning. The visiting by families from the nearby congregations of Indian Creek, Hatfield, Green Tree, Royersford and Coventry, the good sermons by visiting ministers, made the Love Feast occasions memorable times of spiritual fellowship. In the middle and later teens I often went to Love Feasts at Hatfield and Indian Creek, sometimes on my bicycle, and sometimes driving the buggy and taking my sister Esther with me. At

Hatfield we usually stayed with our delightful cousins at Uncle Dan Ziegler's home; at Indian Creek we had good friends who took us home with them.

Our religious experiences were not all in the context of the congregation. My parents taught us from babyhood the kind of behavior expected of Christians. No meal was ever eaten without being blessed by a prayer of thanksgiving. Every morning before breakfast we had a reading from the Bible and knelt by our chairs for prayer. As soon as the children could read, we took our turns reading the daily Bible reading suggested in the Sunday School quarterly. After I was baptized my father occasionally would ask me to lead the prayer. I remember with deep feeling my mother's prayers, very softly spoken, full of love and concern. The first time I left home to go away to school, my father offered the prayer. After this it came to be the pattern that whenever any of us were leaving to go to college, to be married, or to some other new venture, it was always his eloquent and concerned prayer that followed us, across the miles and years.

Our family enjoyed singing. Mother had a beautiful contralto voice and often led the hymns at church. Father sang bass but could not stay on pitch. When a singing school was started in the community, five of our family enrolled; father and mother, my two sisters and I. About sixty persons met two hours one evening a week, and each paid fifteen cents for each session. Our teacher, Eli Wismer, was a lawyer, a fine and competent musician, and organist at a Lutheran church. He was thorough and demanding. We had to learn to read music adequately and to sing good music which was increasingly difficult. The school continued two years; and since about twenty members of the class were from our congregation, the level of our church music vastly improved. In our church we never had choirs or musical instruments. Through this training, we began to use more of the great hymns, and often had ensembles which sang on special occasions.

An incident in our church life still fills me with warmth and gratitude. One year our family had serious financial reverses, with crop shortages and the death of two good cows. Father was hardly able to keep up the modest mortgage payments on the farm. One Sunday Sam Gottshall, one of our deacons, and his wife came to our home for dinner. After the good dinner was over, as we sat in the living room, Sam cleared his throat, and with a note of embarrassment said, "Harry and Mary, we all know that you have been having a bad time. We deacons want to help a little." With that he gave Father an envelope containing $68 in cash! My parents were too choked with emotion to say much. That money would buy two new cows! This kind of sharing concern was typical of our church life, and wild horses could never pull our family away from such a community of love and faith.

I started to school when I was five years and eight months old, walking across the meadow to Linderman's School a half mile from our home. There were about forty pupils in the school, from the little "first reader" children to young men and women in their upper teens. That first year I had a great teacher, Joseph Rosenberry. He had the knack of drawing out the best from every pupil and gave us all much individual attention. Each could go at his own pace. By the end of that year I had completed the third reader! In my second year, a young and inexperienced neighbor woman was the teacher. She put me back to second reader with other children my age. With no new challenges, I turned to all sorts of mischief and was a sore trial to Miss Rhoades. My father talked to her and suggested that she load me with hard work. Soon I was reading many books and exploring arithmetic and history.

My country school career was a checkered one. Some teachers simply "kept school." Others were inspiring and challenging. Miss Marian Bailey taught us to love music, and in our Christmas program we sang the lovely Christmas carols we had just learned. In that program, when I was nine years old, I made my first public speech, a little oration she helped me to prepare on "Useless Giving." Another good teacher was Professor Joseph E. Saylor, who was exactly fifty years older than I. He had been a college professor and was retired without any pension. He was trying to make a living by farming and teaching school. He had a son, little Joe, who was my closest friend all through my growing years. I fear that we children gave Professor Saylor a bad time, for he had an affliction which made him fall asleep in classes and at lunch time, when we would play tricks on him and make his life miserable.

My great interest in reading made me a good speller, too. I won many spelling contests in our school and in the county. I liked geography and my imagination carried me to many far lands. The most interesting extracurricular reading I did was in a weekly paper, *The Youths' Companion*. Its adventure stories, its articles on Indians and wilderness, its tempting offers of premiums for getting new subscribers fired Joe Saylor and me to all kinds of plans for high adventure and perilous journeys. My favorite author in those years was Ernest Thompson Seton, whose wild animal stories and books of nature lore created a whole new world for me. Joe Saylor and I got special delight and inspiration to try many skills from reading his *Two Little Savages*. This was a big book about two boys who learned and practiced all kinds of skills which they learned from the Indians.

Partly because of the books and magazines I read and partly because of my parents' love of the good earth and its creatures, I early developed a life-long interest in birds and flowers. Our farm had many kinds of birds and I found great joy in learning to know them and building nesting boxes for all who cared to use them. Bird watching and keeping careful records of bird migration became my most serious hobby. I also took part in the annual Christmas bird census conducted by the Audubon societies.

We despised and made war on English sparrows and crows. The sparrows were mean and dirty while crows stole eggs, tore up new shoots of corn and were a summer nuisance. But in winter the crows were a delight. Many thousands of them roosted in a woodland a mile from our home. At sunset they came winging in from every direction and in the morning they fanned out over a five-mile radius to forage in the fields. Sometimes they would gather in a big mass meeting in a snow covered field beside the woodland. I sometimes hid nearby to try to discover what their meetings were all about.

Killdeers made their nondescript nests in our potato patch. If we were lucky we might see the tiny, fluffy gray chicks scatter behind small clods within an hour after they hatched. Among the most thrilling memories of strange or unusual birds are these: a pair of redheaded woodpeckers methodically stealing corn from my planting bucket and tucking it in crevices in an old cedar tree for future feasts; the wild "free -freeeee" of upland plovers soaring almost out of sight over our back field or standing like statues on fence posts; a startling albino grackle — a white black-bird totally acceptable to his iridescent black brothers; the haunting and thrilling goose music as ragged V's of Canada geese winged high overhead in spring or fall; a rare American loon fishing in a neighbor's pond; and one bitter cold January evening a huge Arctic Snowy Owl swooping down to catch a rabbit for supper.

I was equally enthralled by the variety and beauty of wild flowers on our farm and in the nearby woodlands of the Stone Hills. For several years I worked at making a collection of pressed wild flowers in an herbarium.

As I began reading the New Testament with deeper interest in my teens, I was delighted with Jesus' keen awareness of all aspects of the natural world, too. He knew the birds, the lilies of the field, the skies, the clouds, the winds. I am sure I felt closer to God in observing these same things.

With all my fascination with wildlife, I do not think I was a loner. Joe Saylor shared my enthusiasm for wild things, and whenever we could we hiked the countryside together, watching birds and exploring the woodlands and meadows for flowers. I never cared for baseball, because I went home for lunch while my schoolmates played ball. Usually I had many chores to do after school. A few of us who came from Brethren homes felt ostracized by other youth our age who were Lutheran or Reformed. They thought we were queer because of our plain dress, our baptism and feetwashing. A sizable group of us grew up together in our church. We were always together at church on Sundays, and usually played together Sunday afternoons, swimming, skating, or playing games. We grew up before the days of radio or TV, and our church frowned on moving pictures or amusement parks. Nor did we have Sunday school picnics. Yet I look back on many joyous times and I never felt deprived. When I was nine or ten, the bigger boys of the community built a fine dam across Lodle Creek in Hunsicker's meadow. They felled an old cherry tree so the trunk spanned the stream, then piled branches against it and built a thick wall of earth and rocks. This gave us a good swimming pool six feet deep, and we used it every warm evening during the summer and skated on it in winter.

The summer I was fourteen a wealthy man bought the meadow and built a strong stone dam forming a full acre of lake. This gave us an even better place for swimming and skating, even attracting fish and wild ducks. Shortly before we left the farm I determined I would go swimming every night after the chores were done, as long as I could. My last dip was in mid-November, when I cracked the thin ice with my head as I dived in. I have never wanted to be a polar bear since then!

At thirteen I graduated from public school. Graduation was at tenth grade level. Commencement was a momentous time, with exercises for the whole township held in the fine old Lutheran-Reformed church at Limerick Center. Of the twenty-five who graduated, most went on to high school at Collegeville the next September. I did not go, for Father thought if I were going to be a dairy farmer as I then planned, high school would not be of much value. So the next three years I worked at home, carrying a man's share of the work on the farm and working with my Uncle Howard threshing and filling silos. In the winter I read a great deal and trapped small animals, selling their furs. One year I saved nearly two hundred dollars from this activity.

Uncle Howard Ziegler and I worked very hard during the summer months doing custom threshing and silo-filling. Earning two dollars a day was attractive. Silo-filling was very strenuous work. In a good corn year we could fill our big wooden silo with eighty tons of corn silage from four acres in one day. Cutting the fifteen foot stalks, piling them on wagons, then pulling them off the load to feed into the hungry jaws of the big silage blower, was exhausting work. But when the twelve men it took to carry on this operation sat down to a dinner table loaded with delicious and bountiful country cooking, the food and good talk made the day seem like a picnic!

The farm tasks I enjoyed most were picking apples in autumn to put in cold storage and harvesting corn. When field corn was ripe we cut it and made orderly rows of shocks to let it dry. Fields with long rows of corn shocks, often dotted with huge yellow pumpkins, were picturesque sights. After a few weeks husking began. We would pull down four shocks in a cluster, husk out the golden ears and throw them in a gleaming pile in the center. The fodder was bundled and hauled to the barn for feed and bedding for the stock in winter. Each evening we would load the ears into a wagon and store them in our airy corn crib.

Though I sometimes rebelled against the incessant work on the farm, I now know that the stern disciplines and the sense of urgency in seed-time and harvest helped me to form invaluable habits of self-discipline and a deep appreciation of the rewards of work well done.

With our diversified and intensive farming and marketing there was too much work on our farm for one man and a growing boy. In the early years Uncle Henry Hunsberger, my mother's younger brother, lived and worked with us. About eighteen when he first came with us, he stayed about five years until he married a beautiful girl, Sadie Bowers, the daughter of a River Brethren bishop who lived near by. They set up their own home, but he continued to work on our farm another year.

Our most colorful hired man was Frank (Bob) Evans, a neighborhood character, a bachelor who had been badly crippled in a fall when he was a boy. Because he never had corrective surgery he walked with great pain. For years he made a meager living by selling produce he bought in a Philadelphia wholesale market, peddling it from his wagon in our community. I especially remember his selling fish, oysters, and bananas. He came to work for us and lived with us after Uncle Henry left. Bob was at his best working with horses, and was an expert at packing big loads of hay or grain. At many tasks such as picking potatoes he was most comfortable working on his knees. This man was a creative story teller. I have never known anyone who could manufacture and tell so many tall tales! He could hold a group spellbound and in stitches of laughter with his preposterous stories of hunting, fishing and travel. Always a perfect gentleman around women, he was master of a store of raunchy stories which he would tell gleefully to men and boys. I must confess that his stories, both funny and dirty, are still hidden in my mental attic, though I never tell the obscene ones.

A welcome visitor to our home two or three times a year was a chubby black-bearded Russian Jew peddler named Hyman Sachs. In the early years, he walked from his home in Norristown carrying his eighty-pound pack on his back and staying at night wherever anyone would lodge him. Usually he was required to sleep in a barn, but at our house my mother always gave him a good supper and a comfortable couch in the living room. Soon he bought a horse and wagon and brought two or three big packs. When he opened his packs after supper and spread out his wares, the family gathered around to see his dress lengths of fine cloth, small articles of clothing, and trays of sundry household items. Sometimes he would tell us stories of the "Old Country" in his broken English. As I recall him now I am reminded of Tevye in "Fiddler on the Roof." Because of the kindly welcome he always received at our home, he frequently said to my mother, "Mary, you good vooman! You will go to Himmel!"

By the time I was fifteen, my plans for the future began to change dramatically. It was the last year of World War I. Many young men of our neighborhood had gone off to the war. My Uncle Robert, then twenty-one, took non-combatant service and was sent to France in the Signal Corps. Though there was great pressure on members of the peace churches, my grandfather steadfastly preached peace, and advised the members of the church not to buy so called Liberty Bonds. Some young Brethren and many Mennonites refused to bear arms at all, and we heard that they were often treated with exasperated and vicious brutality by officers in the army camps.

A month before my sixteenth birthday I started working in factories, first in a steel mill, then in a bottle factory. At the latter place I worked a night shift, driving a horse and buggy to Royersford, four miles away, and working from five o'clock to two in the morning. I worked with old glass blowers as a "snap-up boy" for a while, then helped to run a machine that turned out five hundred dozen pint bottles in a shift. The work was hot and heavy, but I saved up good money to further my new dream of going to college. At two o'clock each morning I hitched old Jim, and slept while he plodded homeward. One rainy morning I woke up and found we were at a strange place. Jim had gotten hungry and perhaps lost and was contentedly chewing fodder from a neighbor's stack, a mile from home!

I saved enough money working in factories, threshing, husking corn and trapping to get me started in Elizabethtown College in December 1919. At that time most students, like myself, were not high school graduates. We took high school subjects and "pedagogical" courses to prepare for teaching school, in the academy. Only a few students were actually on college level. Going off to college was a challenging adventure for me. Now my ambition was to become a teacher. So I plunged into the stimulating ferment of new subjects, some inspiring teachers, and a busy student community life.

My first roommate, Roy K. Miller, a student minister, introduced me to a group called The Student Volunteer Band, many of whom hoped to be foreign missionaries. At least ten of this group did later spend some time as missionaries. We had weekly meetings to study about missions, and the group sent off deputation teams into churches all over Eastern and Southern Pennsylvania to give programs. Before my first year was over I had my first experience on such a team, presenting programs in Hanover and East Berlin, Pennsylvania.

Dating, which we then called "having social privileges," was also a new experience for me. We could walk together, properly chaperoned of course by a lady teacher with a watchful eye, to the Church of the Brethren in Elizabethtown for an evening service. Better yet, we might go to teach Sunday school classes on Sunday afternoon at Newville, three miles away. We were allowed to spend an hour after the Saturday night Literary Society meetings chatting with girls in the Society hall. My first date was with a quiet but pleasant and witty girl from York County, to an evening church service. Later this girl became my sister-in-law, and we are still good friends nearly sixty years later!

After this first year at Elizabethtown, I worked hard on the farm through the summer and fall, earning money to go back to school. That was when we sold the farm and the family moved to Shamokin, where my father would be pastor. He was then forty years old and there were five children in the family. It was indeed a courageous move.

The Shamokin church had been started by my great-grandfather, Daniel P. Ziegler, many years earlier, but it had never prospered. There was no other Church of the Brethren nearer than thirty miles or more across several mountain ranges. Shamokin was a coal mining and manufacturing town of twenty thousand population. The congregation was small and weak, but the District Mission Board had built a beautiful and substantial little church building and paid the pastor's slender salary. I think my father received a hundred dollars a month and had to provide his own house and all other expenses. My mother was frightened and unhappy about the move, but tried to establish a good home in this strange mountain town. When the winter term started I went back to Elizabethtown.

Soon I found new interests and friends. We were assigned places at table in the dining room. At my corner table that winter there were a brother and sister, Foster and Ilda Bittinger from West Virginia. I found them to be serious, sensitive, quiet and deeply religious. Within a week I had asked Ilda for a date. I liked her immensely and planned to take her to the Chautauqua lecture the day after Christmas vacation to hear Russell Conwell give his famous "Acres of Diamonds" lecture.

In the meantime there was tragic news from home. My beautiful sixteen-year-old sister Esther developed scarlet fever. Three days later she died. My father called me and I went home for her funeral. I could not enter the home. After the funeral I went sadly back to school. My little brother Jesse, seven years old, caught the dread disease and nearly died. When I came home for Christmas I also became ill, and missed the first week of college after the holidays. I also missed my date with Ilda and we did not renew our friendship until late in the spring. During the next month I had a profound and life-transforming spiritual experience.

E. B. Hoff, co-founder and co-president of Bethany Bible School, came to Elizabethtown to conduct a Bible Institute and to preach to the students. A wave of religious emotion and dedication swept over the entire student body. Hoff's scholarly but intensely devotional and interesting talks made the Bible and the call to follow Christ in life and service very real and persuasive. My own reaction was a deep new commitment and a resolve to prepare for the ministry of the Gospel, possibly to be a foreign missionary. This was a real conversion experience, a most significant step toward a rewarding life of discipleship and service.

CHAPTER 2

Heir of Promised Grace

Since Alex Haley published his superb story of Kunta Kinte and his descendants, from the West African village of Juffure through generations of slavery to a cultured black family in our time, there has arisen a powerful interest in roots among all families. In the past months my children have quizzed me about our own family roots. Because most people want to know, "Where do you come from? What is your background?" I shall tell about some of my ancestors who have largely formed my heritage.

Philip Ziegler came to America about 1746 from Berne, Switzerland. He received a grant of land from the William Penn heirs in upper Berks County, Pennsylvania, near the long forested range of the Blue Mountain, on Little Swatara Creek. This farm, somewhat smaller now, is still in the Ziegler family. Some years later he or his son gave a parcel of land to the Brethren congregation for a meeting house and cemetery. The building, enlarged and rebuilt, has been known as the Ziegler meeting house, and was one of four houses of worship of the flourishing Little Swatara congregation. A few years ago, the congregation built a beautiful central edifice on a hill near Bethel and abandoned the old-fashioned meeting houses. The Ziegler house was sold to a Mennonite congregation.

Philip Ziegler and his wife, Regina, were members of the Reformed Church, but soon after settling in America they were baptized into the Church of the Brethren. Many of his descendants have been active church people, among them many leaders and ministers in the church.

I have little information about the first three generations of the family in America. About 1825, John Ziegler and his family moved to Rockingham County, Virginia and established the line of Virginia Zieglers. Among his descendants have been David H. Zigler, a leading elder in the church and author of a history of the Brethren in Virginia; M. R. Zigler, for many years the leader of ecumenical service activities in the church; and Earl M. Zigler, a long term missionary in India.

My great-grandfather was Daniel Peiffer Ziegler, great-grandson of Philip. Born March 14, 1823, he lived most of his life near the old homestead. He was a farmer preacher, and a noted healer. In the course of his ministry he walked many miles across the Pennsylvania mountains, preaching and healing. He married twice and had eighteen children. I well remember my great-grandfather, a strong, alert, white-bearded figure, well in his eighties.

Grandfather Jesse Ziegler was born on July 18, 1856. When he was nineteen he moved to Whiteside County, Illinois, where a colony of Pennsylvania Brethren families lived. He married Hannah Horning on April 6, 1879. Here he worked as a carpenter and school teacher. Three sons were born to them there: Samuel on January 11, 1880; my father, Harry, on December 14, 1880; and Warren on June 5, 1882. In 1884 the family moved to Berks County, Pennsylvania, and the next year Grandfather bought his uncle Abraham Conner's farm near Royersford. Here three more sons were born. The family became active in the Mingo Church nearby. In 1890 Grandfather was called to the ministry, and was ordained as an elder in 1900.

My grandfather was a good farmer and a careful business man. He was president of a fertilizer company and a bank director. But above all he was a churchman. He served two years as a pastor, and was for many years the elder of the home church and other congregations as well.

About the turn of the century Brethren leaders in eastern Pennsylvania became deeply interested in higher education. In 1898 they founded a school at Elizabethtown in Lancaster County, which would preserve the conservative lifestyle of the Brethren. Grandfather served as president of the Board of Trustees until his death in 1918 and devoted much time to raising funds for the college and recruiting students. He was a good preacher who combined thorough knowledge of the Bible with compassion and a gentle, dignified pulpit presence. As an elder in the church he was in great demand as a reconciler and carried many district responsibilities.

Grandmother was quick of temper, even what today we would call feisty. She lived to be well past ninety. After she was widowed in 1918, she took up china painting, and the beautiful dishes she painted are a treasured heirloom in her grandchildren's homes.

The last five years of Grandfather's life he was crippled by a painful bone disease, which put him on crutches. He and Grandmother bought a home in Limerick, near us, and I became their handyman and coachman, keeping up their lawn and garden, and driving their horse Jerry whenever they went to church or elsewhere.

Grandmother Ziegler's father, Samuel Eisenberg Horning, was born October 23, 1831. He lived to a great age, about 91. As a young man he had gone west to Illinois, where he became an expert in building and moving barns and houses. At one time, after Great Grandmother's death in 1885, he homesteaded land in Wisconsin and could tell tales of wolves howling around his log cabin at night. When he was past eighty he spent a winter with us and built for my father a beautiful desk-bookcase combination of fine walnut, cherry and poplar wood, now an heirloom in our family. We children were entranced by his stories of "spooks," wolves, and his adventures moving barns in Illinois. When we knew him he had a deep lateral crease in his bald head which he said was caused by a big 8 x 10 oak timber falling on his head while he was building.

My father was a farmer-preacher and a scholar. He made the living for his growing family by intensive farming until he was 40. Then he was a pastor for twelve years, first in Shamokin, Pennsylvania, then in Ridgely, Maryland. He found pastoral work difficult, although he was a strong preacher and teacher. The care of souls was not easy, and he could be sharp and outspoken in his judgments of people. In Shamokin he received $100 per month, from which he paid his own rent, cared for his family, and all incidental expenses. I believe he also served as janitor of the church.

In Ridgely he bought a small farm, drove a school bus, and received a small salary. He soon was at odds with some older leaders of the church. When the depression came, he lost the farm, left the pastorate, and moved to Talbot County near Easton, Maryland. He served in the free ministry of the Fairview Church and built up a business selling Rawleigh Company products in the county. This business flourished, and when he retired from it after twenty-five years, he had a small comfortable home and adequate resources for the retired years.

Dad was a Bible student. When he was seventeen years old he was elected teacher of the adult Bible class in the Mingo Church. Wherever he lived, including the two churches he served as pastor, he continued teaching adult classes. When he was about eighty he became totally blind, but continued teaching. When he finally gave up his class he had taught seventy-one years without interruption!

In my growing years I loved, respected and resented my father. He was rather stern and short-tempered as a parent, and insisted on unquestioning obedience. As his eldest child, I bore the brunt of his learning how to be a good father. I began to help with farm chores very early, learned to milk cows by the age of nine, and from then on he gave me more and more responsibilities. By the age of fourteen I was doing a grown man's work. If I dawdled, or neglected my tasks, Dad became impatient and sometimes exasperated. He believed that sparing the rod would spoil the child, so I got many whippings—with a paddle or strap, or whatever was handy.

On the other hand, Dad taught me to love the Bible, to enjoy good books, and would often give me half days off from farm work for my nature study pursuits. I think he was quietly proud of my interests, and after I started to college he gave me some small financial help which he could ill afford. Dad was concerned about my growing into adolescence. While we were cutting corn together when I was about twelve, he told me about sex and how babies came into the world. I vividly recall his telling me once that a man must be very considerate and temperate in his relations with his wife; that he and my mother did not consummate their marriage until three months after the wedding! It must have been good then, because I was born just a year and two weeks after they were married! Dad warned me, too, about masturbation; he believed that the practice of "self-abuse" would lead to insanity and possibly inability to have children. Of course, he was not alone in this kind of illusion; many doctors taught the same thing then!

But like most other youngsters, I had other sources of sex education. And I failed, as ninety-nine per cent of other boys my age did, to heed his warnings. Nevertheless, the high standards of reverence for women, chastity, and consideration which he taught me were to stay with me. And when I came to marriage, I was very glad that my bride and I had to learn intimacy together!

Dad had a tender and kindly side, too. I never heard him utter an unkind word to my gentle mother in the fifty-seven years of their married life. Nor would he permit her to do the kind of outdoor farm chores which so many neighbor women had to do. And after exercising a fairly stern discipline in my upbringing, he became more and more gentle, kind and even indulgent with the younger children. I often protested that, though he had disciplined me severely, my brother Jesse, ten years younger, never was whipped! At first he used to say that Jesse behaved better than I did. But in his later years he cheerfully admitted that he had learned much better ways of nurturing children as the years went on.

My father's brothers all influenced my growing years in varied ways. Uncle Sam was a teacher for fifty years, getting his graduate degrees and writing several books while teaching in high schools and colleges. He inspired me in my nature studies and urged me to go to college. His sharp cool criticism in my teaching and preaching ministry was stimulating.

Uncle Howard was the farmer. Uncle Warren worked for the Brethren Publishing House more than forty years, often in charge of the book sales at Annual Conference. Uncle Robert was only seven years older than I. He had hoped to be a minister but died young as a result of gas injuries while he was in France.

I know far too little of my ancestors on Mother's side. They were solid German-speaking Mennonites. I well remember her parents, her

Uncle David Bergey, and a few cousins. Her grandfather, Isaac Bergey, died in 1860, leaving nine young children, of whom Grandmother was the youngest. All of them were still living in 1891, when they held a family reunion. Uncle David Bergey was blind in one eye, for an owl had swooped down when he found her nest in his orchard and so badly scratched his face that he lost the sight of one eye.

My mother, the eldest of her family, was born February 23, 1879. Her two brothers and two sisters all followed her into the Church of the Brethren. Her younger sister, Elizabeth, lived with us until she married in her late thirties. Though mother's later years were marred by ill health, she out-lived all her brothers and sisters.

She was a beautiful woman. Like my father, she had not gone beyond grade school. But she had a good mind, great love of beauty and music, and a gentle spirit. Though she bore and reared seven children, and in our farm years had few household conveniences, I cannot remember her ever seeming frantic or rushed. And even though cooking, washing, cleaning, caring for little children, gardening and putting up dried and canned foods for winter must have kept her very busy, she always had beautiful house plants in winter and a profusion of garden flowers in summer. She loved music, could play hymns on our parlor organ, and often was singing about the house.

She never travelled far, but she loved people and the beauty of the world around her. Her appreciation of beauty and of God's created world rubbed off on all of us children. Perhaps my own great interest in birds and flowers, in books and music I owe very directly to her, though the love of reading comes even more powerfully from my father.

I was the eldest of seven children. The family doctor who helped me into the world was Dr. Edward Krusen. My parents respected him highly and named me after him. He must have liked the idea, for he put a dollar into a savings account for me. He also ushered my two sisters, Esther and Florence, into the world. Esther was born May 23, 1904. I cannot remember that event! But I do remember that on August 4, 1906, Dr. Krusen came out from our house, climbed into his buggy and said to me, "Eddie, you have another baby sister; be nice to her!" Unfortunately, I wasn't!

My brother Mark was born July 30, 1910, at Green Valley Farm. He was a beautiful blue-eyed baby. When he was one and one-half years old he caught measles, then pneumonia, and died early in the morning of April 14, 1912, the day the Titanic sank. When my sisters and I went to bed, we knew he was very sick. My father came to my bed, wakened me gently and said, "Mark has gone now to be with Jesus." Though we all cried and felt a great sense of loss when Mark left us, I am sure that Dad set the tone of our acceptance of death, and we were not afraid.

On the morning of January 7, 1913, our barnyard was a sheet of ice. I was up in the barn preparing feed for the cattle when I heard my father scream. Our huge Holstein bull had caught him on his horns and was rushing him across the icy yard, bent back over his giant head. On the far side, Dad tumbled through a narrow gap between the woodshed and a heavy rail fence, where the bull could not follow. Mother had just come out of the house and watched in horror. Dad picked himself up, not badly injured, and we managed to get the bull safely chained in the barn!

That evening my brother Jesse was born. We older children had gone from school to Grandma's house, and came back late in the evening to see this tiny red-faced squalling infant in Mother's arms!

On February 15, 1916, another baby girl was born. Her name was Grace Elizabeth. Like Esther, she was pretty, even-tempered, and bright. Since she was only eight when I left home, only three when I went away to school, I never learned to know her well. She always did very well in school, and in September 1934, when she was 18, she went off happily to Bridgewater College, hoping to prepare to be a missionary nurse. During the Thanksgiving holidays she went to Roanoke, Virginia, with a deputation group. On Thanksgiving Day she became very ill and was taken to Lewis Gale Hospital. Soon she was in a deep coma, and two days later she died. Losing two daughters was a very severe loss to my mother and father. The experiences of grief mellowed my father and gave greater depth of compassion to his preaching. Mother's life after this always had an undertone of sadness.

And finally, when I was nineteen and a busy school teacher still living at home, our little sister Mary was born, April 12, 1922. A bright, vivacious and maybe spoiled baby, she filled to a great extent the vast grieving hurt in Mother's heart caused by Esther's death sixteen months earlier. One of my memories of Mary's early years is seeing her escape from Mother in church when she was two, trotting up to the pulpit and holding to Father's leg and smiling at the congregation as he tried to continue his sermon!

As all families must, our family grew up and scattered. When I was twenty-one I married and went to West Virginia. More of that in the next chapter. Let me briefly tell about the other three children.

Florence was a flimsy teen-ager, not well enough to go on to high school. At the age of 19 she married Otto Sanger, a courtly, witty, pint-sized Maryland farmer and orchardist, who was twice her age. Otto and Florence lived the rest of their lives in Talbot County, on the Eastern Shore.

My brother Jesse has spent all his mature years in theological education. After receiving his graduate degrees in psychology, he taught eighteen years in Bethany Theological Seminary. Since 1960, he has been working with the Association of Theological Schools, first as associate, then as executive director. In August 1939 he was married to Harriet Curry, a beautiful, witty Pennsylvanian girl, who graduated from Elizabethtown College. Since 1960 they have lived in or near Dayton,

Ohio. We two brothers have a strong and warm relationship. We occasionally find ourselves on opposite sides of a question in church polity, but both of us have a deep loyalty to the church in which we were nurtured and in whose ministry we have served.

Jesse and I both felt strongly that our younger sister Mary should go to college. Mother was apprehensive about it, and Dad could not afford to pay her way, so we brothers helped her to get started. She graduated from Bridgewater in 1944, majoring in music. That same year she was married to James Lee Houff, a minister from Roanoke, Virginia. He has served in Brethren pastorates in Virginia, Illinois and Florida, and United Methodist churches in Illinois. They are now in North Carolina where James is pastor of the Eden Church of the Brethren.

Mother and Dad built a comfortable little house in Cordova, Maryland, convenient for Dad's good business and close to the little rural Fairview Church which they had come to love. On December 21, 1951, they celebrated their golden wedding anniversary. Jesse and I drove from Chicago — 900 miles over icy roads! We four sons and daughters formed a quartet to provide music for the celebration, and Dad's good friend and colleague, Barry Fox, led in a short but deeply moving ritual.

Mother's health had been precarious for some years before that — a failing heart and some cancer. But she lived on until August 1957, very frail and often forgetful. In her latter years Dad gave up his business, partly because he could no longer see to drive. But he gradually took over all the housework and became a competent cook and housekeeper as well as nurse.

Early in the morning of August 30, 1957, Florence called me on the phone and said, "Mother woke up in Heaven this morning instead of her bed." The beautiful service in the Fairview Church, when her body was laid to rest beside that of our sister Grace, was not a time of sadness but of celebration. She had been a lovely and beautiful person, and the day was filled with joyful, sometimes poignant, sometimes funny memories. All of us had the sure confidence that whatever the next life held for our mother, she was well enough acquainted with God and all beauty, and with her three children who had gone on before her, that she would be very much at home!

Dad sold his home and went to live in a little apartment Otto and Florence had prepared for him in their house at Windy Hill. On the day of Mother's funeral he told me, "I have prayed for two things — that Mother wouldn't have much pain, and that I could keep my sight long enough to care for her properly; both prayers have been granted me!"

Within a few years Dad became totally blind, and lived in physical darkness for ten years. But there was no mental or spiritual darkness. We children put some resources together and bought him the complete Bible on long-playing records. For many years he had read the Bible through twice every year and had memorized great portions of it. Now he could hear it read, and he continued going through it twice a year. He also received expositions of the International Sunday School lessons on records from the John Milton Society for the Blind, as well as a constant stream of books from the Library of Congress on every kind of topic. He wore out more than one record player!

He continued teaching Bible class at Fairview until 1968 and often preached sermons. Occasionally he conducted weddings and funerals, having the rituals by memory. He had accumulated a library of some three thousand books. While he gave some to his children, he gave most of his books to the black ministers in the county. Many of them had become his close friends, and he was sometimes called the bishop of the black churches of the county.

The year after Dad was 87, he flew to California to visit us, where I was then pastor in Bakersfield. Florence saw him to a plane in Baltimore and I met him in Los Angeles. He never had been farther west than Iowa. The month of May he spent with us was a rich experience. He told us he wanted to "see" two things — the Pacific Ocean, and a giant Sequoia tree. So one day we drove a hundred miles to the ocean at Ventura. On the beach he kicked off his shoes and walked toward the sound of the surf until he felt the surge of the little waves over his feet; he had *seen* the Pacific.

Another day we drove up the steep, winding road to the Giant Forest in Sequoia National Park. Though it was late in May, there was deep snow everywhere. I pulled up beside a medium sized Sequoia along the Generals' Highway, a mere sapling some sixteen feet in diameter. Opening the car door, I pointed him toward the tree. He moved to it, spread out his arms as far as he could reach, and laid his cheek against the soft red bark. He considered this one of the high points of his visit.

When I asked him to preach in a morning service he was a bit apprehensive, and perhaps my congregation was, too. But when the time for the sermon came Dad stood erect in the pulpit, flawlessly recited by memory eighteen verses from the Gospel, then preached a well-organized, thoughtful fifteen-minute sermon, summed it up in a few memorable sentences and sat down. Then the congregation breathed again!

Dad lived to be ninety and one-half years old. In his last year he had a succession of small strokes. His last six weeks of life he was in a good nursing home where he made many friends. He took great pride in becoming the oldest Ziegler on record, at least in our Pennsylvania branch of the tribe. Never widely known, as Grandfather had been, my father left a rich heritage. He never stopped growing. As a younger man he adhered to the fundamentalist literal interpretation of the Bible. And he was a bit conservative in politics, always voting Republican. But he kept growing in his theology and his warm human relationships throughout his long and busy life! He was a good minister of Jesus Christ.

I believe one of the best things about our growing years was our being together in work and play and in our religious activities. Though I sometimes chafed about having so much hard work to do, I always knew Dad was working harder than I, and that we were together. One summer Clyde Horner, a boy a year older than I who was a foster child and did not experience the love and warmth I did, thought seriously of running away. We both read Youth's Companion stories of the frontier and the North Woods and dreamed of spending a winter trapping furs in Canada. But the warmth and trust in our home over-balanced my restlessness, and we never went. Then, too, I would never bring myself to hurt Mother! I agreed with old Sachs; she was a good woman, and I didn't want to hasten her departure for Heaven!

CHAPTER 3

Gladly Did I Learn and Gladly Teach

I came to Shamokin to live at home in the summer of 1921. I passed the Teachers' Examination and signed a contract to teach the Owltown School in Irish Valley, five miles north of my home. Then for the summer months I was a day laborer, helping to dig up a city street for a sewer line. It was rugged, hot work, and by the end of the second day my hands were a mass of bleeding blisters. I soon toughened up. Each day I was required to dig with pick and shovel a section of ditch twelve feet long, thirty inches wide and six to eight feet deep, including breaking up and throwing out rocks. When the foreman learned that I could handle a plow, he had me guide the ripper to tear up the asphalt pavement, pulled by a steam roller.

When September came, I was glad to begin my new career as a teacher. Owltown was a one-room brick building about thirty by forty feet at a crossroads beside a small stream. In the middle of the room was a big pot-bellied stove with double desks around it. I found that I had fifty-seven boys and girls in all the eight grades. Most were farm children, with a sprinkling of Polish and Czech children whose fathers were coal miners. The playground was dusty or muddy according to the weather conditions. The children almost all brought their lunches, and on nice days they sat under the trees along the road to eat. Recess times and lunch hours were spent playing ball, or the older ones ranged over the nearby hills playing fox and geese. Nearby there was a well with a rusty old iron pump where we got cool water to fill the big cooler in one corner of the school room. When cold weather came, we fed the stove with bucketfuls of gleaming anthracite coal. On very cold or snowy days when the children came in around the glowing stove with wet clothes and some-times unwashed bodies, the aroma could be rather overpowering! We had no running water, no electric lights. The toilet facilities were a pair of ramshackle, unpainted, wooden outhouses behind the school house, which were cleaned twice a year by the school trustees!

To get to school I could ride three miles on an antiquated trolley car and then walk across a shoulder of the mountain one and a half miles to the school. I usually walked home in fair weather. I was at school by eight every morning, in time to kindle or stir up the fire and be ready to start school at 8:30. When school was out at four o'clock, two or three children often would stay to help sweep and tidy up for the next day. My "portal to portal" day was eleven hours long. I had a comfortable room at my parents' home where my mother's meals were substantial and delicious. I paid five dollars a week for room and board. My salary was seventy-five dollars a month for the seven-month term.

I found that I got along well with children and liked most of them; there were a few conspicuous exceptions! The job was exciting. I had taken several "methods" courses in college, and County School Superin-tendent Swank was kind and helpful. Teaching eight grades in one room sounds frightfully complicated. But I worked out a schedule of rotation of classes, and it was amazing to see how much younger children learned just by listening to the older children reciting. While one group would work at the chalkboards, I would be hearing another class or helping in-dividuals at their desks.

Most of the children were well behaved. One feisty ten-year-old threw a handful of rifle cartridges into the fire one cold day and the explosions almost created a panic. One bullet hit a boy's leg but did little injury. I gave the boy a mild spanking, which greatly incensed an older brother to the point that he came out on the road the next morning and beat me up! One behavior problem was obscene talk which a few boys, and one or two girls, liked to bandy about to shock the other children. I threatened and scolded and occasionally spanked a boy for this talk. Sometimes there would be playground fights with bloody noses and pulled hair. In fact, I once put on boxing gloves with a big boy and got a bloody nose myself, to the amusement of the youngsters. But on the whole it was a busy, happy, creative, successful year.

I taught two more years at Owltown and had a raise in salary to $100 a month and an eight-month term. The school population grew also. The second year I had 62 children, with twelve in first grade, and the third year sixty-seven! I tried to bring a little culture into the community, too. Several of my colleagues in the six one-room schools in the township joined me in getting sets of beautiful lantern slides—the big glass ones—and an acetylene-powered projector from the Pennsylvania Museum. We would put on an evening show twelve or fifteen times a year and pass on the equipment to the next school. At Owltown we also started a monthly literary society, or debating club, which was well attended by older pupils and quite a few parents as well.

Two Polish families, the Buraks, lived in a heavily forested little valley a mile north of the school. The men of the families worked in the coal mines near Shamokin. About seven children came to school from these families, but they were quite irregular in attendance, often staying home to work on their little farms. State attendance laws were strict and both families were fined for illegally keeping their children out of school. The parents were hurt and angry and thought they were being hounded and fined because they were foreigners who spoke poor English. The children were bright, lovable and clean and did very well in school. Near the end of my third and last year at Owltown a dramatic incident occurred with these families.

Spring had come hot and early, and for several weeks no rain had fallen, leaving the forests tinder dry. Forest fires raged along the mountains near the school. One bright, hot April day, a big fire was set by a spark from a locomotive in the pine-clad hills above the Burak farms. When we dismissed for lunch, there was a huge ominous cloud of smoke over their little valley, as the fire roared down the slope toward the buildings. I quickly sent the younger children home while the dozen older boys and I raced across the hill to the farms. The fire was almost to the barns and the mothers were terribly frightened. The boys formed a bucket brigade, while two older boys and I climbed to the roof of the nearest barn to pour water on the smoking shingles as burning brands fell on them. Soon, however, the roof was on fire and then the hay and straw beneath caught fire with a roar. We got out the horse and cows, then ran to save the house. As small blazes started, we were able to contain them. Within fifteen minutes the barn was a heap of smoking ruins, but we saved the house while the fire roared up the opposite hillside and burned out in an open field. The boys and I had a few small burns and holes burned in our shirts and pants.

When just a few days later we held our "last day of school" picnic for the children and their families, the Polish families not only came, but they insisted on providing two huge freezers of home-made ice cream for the whole crowd!

Though Owltown School has long been closed and consolidated with others, until recently the building was still standing, a refuge for wasps, squirrels and bats, and some old rusting farm machinery. A narrow paved road now winds over the hill behind the school house, and the sleepy little valley is still inhabited by some sturdy Pennsylvania Dutch farmers and a few families who make their living in the little city beyond the mountain.

At the time I began teaching, I was considering another important decision. Because of the profound spiritual awakening I had at Elizabethtown I felt more and more drawn to the ministry, and possibly to foreign mission service. I talked about this with my father and with Elder "Uncle Sam" Hertzler, who was like a grandfather to me. On November 26, 1921, Uncle Sam and Elder Isaac W. Taylor, both revered leaders in the Eastern Pennsylvania District and members of the District Ministerial Board, came to our church in Shamokin. They talked long with me about my vocation, then in a congregational council they took the vote of the congregation for my call to the ministry. I was ordained in that same evening meeting. The simple dignity and the solemn ritual of ordination, the awesome feeling of divine call when the elders laid their hands on my head and prayed as I knelt before them, remain among my most treasured memories. Shortly before my nineteenth birthday, I was made a minister of the Gospel!

Though I had frequently gone with deputation teams from Elizabethtown College, I preached my first formal sermon in the Shamokin Church on Christmas morning, 1921. My subject was "The Angels' Message" (Luke 2:10-14). After the service, while Dad and I were sitting in his study at home waiting for Mother to finish preparing our Christmas dinner, Dad asked with a smile, "Do you remember that that was the same text I used for my first sermon two years ago on Christmas Day at Mingo?" I was ashamed to say that I had not remembered the sermon. I did remember how he looked, however. He had a broken, grotesquely swollen nose from an encounter with a flying ten-gallon steel milk can!

From this time on I preached occasionally in the church and at the farm home of an elderly couple who lived six miles out in the mountains where we held monthly Sunday afternoon meetings. The church elected me Sunday School superintendent also, and though there were only about thirty members of the church we had many children in Sunday School. Many of them came from non-church homes in the community. For three years I taught a class of six- to eleven-year-old children in the balcony of the church. I had over forty children enrolled in this class and was tempted to pray for bad weather so they couldn't all come! I have often wondered how much good we did these children. We had little contact with their homes. Many of them came from homes where the parents chased them off to church while they recovered from Saturday night hangovers in a welter of empty beer cans and Sunday papers.

There were only two or three other persons of my age in our church membership. The closest friends I had were two young women. One was a tall, dark, quiet girl, Madeline, who lived in Sunbury, twenty miles away, and came with her mother quite regularly to our church. Dating Madeline meant a train trip Saturday afternoon, hikes along the Susquehanna River or visiting in her home, then a late night train ride back home so I could be in my post in church on Sunday morning. I think we were never much in love and never discussed marriage. The other close friend was a bright, red-haired Lutheran girl who lived near us and taught a one-room school near Irish Valley. Verna and I had much in common, sharing many religious and professional interests. Since our church had no youth organization, I found the Luther League in Verna's church a most congenial group and went with her to many of their activities.

It might seem almost ludicrous to modern youth for me to report that I never kissed either of these girls! The kind of strict standards which prevailed at our college and the teaching about boy-girl relationships prevalent then dictated that a couple might hold hands but that they never kissed until they were engaged. I have reason to believe that many of my contemporaries, even fellow students, weren't quite so restrained in their behavior!

As soon as my school term was over in April, I returned to Elizabethtown for the special six-week spring term for teachers and a six- or eight-week intensive summer term, both in 1922 and 1923. Study was intensive; I took two years of Latin in fourteen weeks! I plunged into other activities eagerly. It seemed wonderful to be back among a swarm of other Brethren young people. I again took an active part in Student Volunteer deputation work, preaching in such churches as Ephrata, Palmyra, and York. One person I was particularly eager to see again was Ilda Bittinger, whom I had learned to know well the year before. By the end of the 1921 school year she and I had had several dates. The Brethren Annual Conference was at Hershey that June and I served as usher. Ilda also attended the Conference, and I escorted her to her rooming place each night. I did not tell her that my only pair of shoes was too tight and that I stopped by a little stream to soak my blisters in the cool water before going back to my own room.

Ilda spent the summer of 1921 as a home mission worker deep in the Allegheny mountains at a place called Onego, fifty miles from her home. Many of the people there were rather primitive, and she was lonely. A few weeks after she started work there, she wrote me a long letter. It was cordial, full of good talk and stories about her work and the place and people. On a corner of the first page she had attached a beautiful, delicate pressed columbine. I had never had such a letter from any girl, and it was a splendid event in my life. We kept up a sporadic correspondence through the year and both of us were ready for some good dating when I returned to the campus in April.

I think we were greatly attracted to each other by our mutual appreciation of wild life, by our interests in faith and in music and poetry. We took long walks during the June week between terms, when there was no watchful chaperone to guard us. One incident during the summer term was both funny and embarrassing. That summer the girl students were under the watchcare of a nervous and extremely conscientious teacher who seemed to be in deadly fear that one of her girls might be kissed! On July 4, the students organized a picnic and corn roast at a famous and rare prostrate juniper tree in the hills near Hershey. It was a delightful party, though Miss M. brooded over us like an anxious hen. We were to be back at the college by ten o'clock. This involved being on the nine o'clock trolley from Hershey, then a mile walk back to the campus. Three of us who were student ministers and our girls volunteered to take the baskets of sweet corn that were left over back to the farm where we had bought it, a half mile beyond the picnic spot. The main party went on with Miss M. to catch the trolley. When we came back by the picnic place, we found our campfire still burning. Like good scouts, we stopped to put out the fire, carefully, but not hastily, then went on to catch up with the group. Alas, we had missed the trolley, and poor Miss M. was on the verge of tears. She had sent the rest of the party on home, and waited for us. It was eleven o'clock when we got back to college.

The next morning at six o'clock I was called to the dormitory phone. President J.G. Meyer was on the line, curtly summoning me to an immediate conference in his office. I dutifully appeared. Miss M. had reported our outrageous behavior to him as soon as she got back to the campus and the honor of the college was at stake! I never knew why I was the first of the three culprits to be summoned to the judgment seat, but I got the full blaze of the president's righteous wrath. Our lame excuse about having to put out the campfire was too lame indeed. I had lied, deeply hurt a fine conscientious professor, had flouted the noble standards of the college, compromised the honor of a pure young girl, was unworthy of being a minister, et cetera, et cetera, ad nauseam! The other two young men, one of them the president's younger brother, got off with shorter lectures, for it was breakfast time. The three girls involved were campused for a month and we were forbidden dates for the same period.

By the end of that summer, however, Ilda and I were again seeing each other, even having some beautiful clandestine moonlight walks. The evening before we were to leave campus, since school was out, we were under no further restrictions. We rode the trolley to Hershey and spent a long evening strolling, talking and admiring the lovely gardens and flowers around the old Hershey mansion. Before we were to start home I told Ilda of the great love for her which I had felt growing all summer and asked her if she could possibly consider marrying me and sharing my life. When she said Yes, we kissed for the first time. It was a beautiful moment, but I was inexperienced and landed my first kiss on her nose before we found each other's lips.

On our way back to the campus we talked deeply about our future. Both of us were committed to ministry in the church, but she had no thought of becoming an ordained minister. We agreed that we would wait two years for marriage so that I could teach two more years and reach the age of twenty-one. She would have a brief vacation at home at Eglon, West Virginia, and then return to college. We would spend the Christmas holidays at her home.

From that time on our letters were much more frequent and were full of eager planning, exploring each other's thinking, sharing visions and dreams for our future. I managed to make the three-hour train trip to Elizabethtown several times during the year. When Christmas vacation came, we would travel to her home by the slow, scenic route of the Western Maryland Railroad. I almost missed the trip, however. My father had a stubborn, severe cough, and two days before vacation he came down with a dangerous case of pneumonia. The next day he wished to be anointed. I was the only Brethren minister within forty miles, and I had never even seen an anointing service. But Father said, "Call Lewis Paul (one of our deacons) and I will tell you how to do it." Deacon Paul came right after his work day and together we conducted the service. At that moment the fever was very high and Father was a very sick man. I offered to cancel my trip, but he would not hear of it, assuring us he would soon be well again.

Early in the morning before leaving, I slipped into his bedroom to see how he was. The fever had gone and he was resting well. His recovery was swift and complete. I left, and three days later received a letter from him, telling me he was up and feeling fine!

I met Ilda in Harrisburg, and we rode all day, arriving long after dark at a little station in West Virginia called William. Her father and two brothers met us in their Model T Ford, and soon we were at her farm home. The week there was memorable. The Bittinger farm was on the Allegheny Plateau, a mile from the little hamlet of Eglon. The winter weather was much colder than I had known in Pennsylvania. It did not take long to get acquainted with the family. Her father Jonas was a sturdy, black-bearded, taciturn man, a good farmer and a conscientious deacon in the Maple Spring Church. Her mother, Etta Fike, was ambitious for her family, very frugal, progressive in her views about religion and education. Had she been a man, she would have been a strong, influential elder!

Ilda was the eldest in the family. Her brother Foster, whom I had learned to know at Elizabethtown two years earlier, was now a junior at Bridgewater College and already a minister also. William, my own age, was the farmer of the family. Curly-haired Desmond, thoughtful and sensitive, was a high school senior. Playford, the tallest and handsomest of the four boys, was an ardent woodsman and follower of Tarzan. Little sister Ruth, seven years old, followed me around with eyes as big as saucers, usually lugging a cat so big its tail dragged on the floor. I didn't pass her inspection very well, for I didn't seem to care for her cats.

The Maple Spring Church was the center of the community life. It was outstanding. There were at least ten ministers in the congregation, who served five or six preaching points within a ten-mile radius. At that time six of the ministers were Fikes: John, Jonas, Ezra, Moses (Ilda's grandfather), Lorenzo and Emra. Another fine minister was Dr. Harold Miller, a dedicated and brilliant physician who came back to practice in his home community and who constantly stirred intense intellectual fires in the younger people. There were several student ministers coming on also. Dr. Miller's wife, Blanche Bonsack Miller, was also a fine physician, and the couple had a tremendous compassionate ministry of healing, based in a large wing of their comfortable old stone house, "Gilead."

Each year at Christmas time the church had a week-long Bible Institute. There were morning and afternoon sessions, with a fantastic basket dinner between sessions. These meetings were lively, with young people and local ministers giving talks and leading discussions, and good singing. Each year a strong popular guest minister was invited to give Bible lectures and to preach inspirational or evangelistic sermons in the evening meetings. That year Marshall Wolfe, a local young man doing his graduate work in Bethany Bible School, was the preacher. The high quality of most sessions, the good Koinonia fellowship and the total absence of outside distractions made these weeks a period of vigorous growth and celebration for the entire community. And everyone came! When the snow was deep, a usual condition, most families came in two-horse bob-sleds; in cars only if they had chains. Coming from our tiny city congregation and hearing only my father's preaching, these institutes were a truly mind-stretching experience for me, even though I was preoccupied with courting. Often Ilda and I walked to and from the meetings through the snow, taking a short cut through the big sugar maple trees to Eglon and the church.

That was a wonderful week! I think the Bittinger family approved of me. Ilda was a popular young woman in the community, and her neighbors really sized me up. I suspect many of her aunts and cousins were a bit distrustful of this young city teacher/preacher who wanted to carry her off.

The end of the week brought high adventure. One of Foster's Bridgewater instructors, Professor Starr, had left his Overland touring car in the Bittinger barn, taking the train from Oakland to his home in Ohio. He was to arrive on an evening train on the Baltimore and Ohio Railway to Oakland on December 30. The weather had turned warm and most roads were a sea of mud. Foster, Ilda and I drove a roundabout way to Oakland to meet the professor. He did not come on the eight-o'clock train so we decided to wait for the next train at two in the morning. To pass the time we went to a boring movie. At eleven o'clock the town sidewalks were rolled up and we waited in the station. But our man did not arrive then either. So we started home. Foster thought the mud roads would be frozen hard by now, so he took a short cut. Alas, we soon bogged down in axle-deep freezing mud, six miles from home. We pushed, lifted, pulled, shoved, even prayed, to no avail. So leaving the car we walked home, arriving at sunrise, completely exhausted. In fact, I went to sleep walking, and had we not been supporting each other I would have landed in the ditch.

Later in the day the Bittinger horses pulled the car out, and once more Foster went to Oakland and found his professor. Early on January 1, Father Bittinger took the four of us, including two of Ilda's student cousins, in the spring wagon to the paved road and we started in the professor's car for Hagerstown. But the adventure was not yet over. The car had no heater. And on the first high mountain on the old National Road, at the top of Negro Mountain, we skidded around on a stretch of ice and the windshield crashed in a thousand pieces. We drove on six more hours in the freezing wind, crossing many mountains. Finally, four miles west of Hagerstown the car gave up. We walked to Hagerstown carrying our baggage. Ilda, her cousins and I took a train to Harrisburg. There we parted. They went on to Elizabethtown, and I arrived in Shamokin long after midnight, ready(?) to start teaching at eight-thirty the next morning!

During the three years that I lived in Shamokin I was drawn into a group of dedicated but extremely conservative Christian business and professional men from several churches. They had weekly Bible study meetings and occasionally made forays into evangelism. The leader of the group, Gus Steinhart, was a middle-aged, hard-driving businessman, a member of the Plymouth Brethren sect. My closest friend in the group was a young optician, Dr. Billig, who had invited me into the group. Their theological stance included a strong emphasis on premillenialism, with an eager expectation of the imminent return of Christ. I bought a Scofield Reference Bible and for a time was carried away by their enthusiasm, attending many of their meetings. My father also knew this theological stance, but he and I both began to be wary of it. While I was soon turned off by their extremism, the emphasis upon intense Bible study and faithful discipleship have been a strong legacy to me. Fortunately, the Bible classes I took at Elizabethtown, and more importantly later at Bridgewater, gave me a much more solid and orthodox biblical theology to live by.

Through these busy years I did not lose my early interest in wild life and nature study. I found it impossible to lounge on Saturdays and took many long hikes into the surrounding mountains and valleys. I found a place where intensely blue fringed genians grew along a roadside near my school. On the tops of limestone ridges near where we had Sunday afternoon meetings, I found many kinds of marine fossils. And always there were myriads of birds.

These were rich, busy, growing years. I thoroughly enjoyed teaching school and found the occasional opportunities for preaching an increasing challenge. Several times I was invited to preach in churches of other denominations in the area. For a while, several young people from the Luther League and I conducted monthly services in an abandoned Baptist Church out in the country. But few people came, and we abandoned the project.

The spring and summer terms at Elizabethtown were intense and refreshing. I earned enough credits so that I had a strong equivalency diploma and eight semester-hour credits when I entered my regular college course later on. I was learning to enjoy good music. For several months I had voice lessons from a fine teacher who had been a soprano in the Metropolitan Opera before marrying and moving to Shamokin, where I had her two lively youngsters in my school.

Ilda and I planned to be married on May 31, 1924. We were invited by the District Mission Board to settle at Onego in Pendleton County, West Virginia, where I would be pastor of the Seneca Congregation and teach school. In a between-term vacation in 1923, I went to Onego to conduct a week's "revival meeting." Father Bittinger drove me to the railway and I rode many miles on the slow log train to Harman. Then I walked ten miles across the Allegheny Mountain to Onego. I enjoyed one of the best meals of my life at the home of Deacon Abe Cunningham before meeting that evening. His wife, Pearlie, had fried big black bass which Abe had just caught in the Seneca Creek and served them with new potatoes and peas from their garden, topping it all off with a huge slab of cherry pie smothered in pure fresh cream! I preached five evenings at Onego and found these mountain people friendly, though a bit suspicious of so young a preacher. There was an epidemic of measles in the community, so I did not stay my full week. But it was long enough to give me an eager anticipation of making our first home there, where we would begin a life of ministry together.

CHAPTER 4

We Face Life Together

"How long does it take to make a good marriage?" asked Dr. Henrietta Wieman in a stimulating class on marriage and family in which I was enrolled one summer at Garrett Biblical Seminary. "You can't get married in one day. If you are two morons, you can achieve such a degree of marriage as morons are capable of in from two to five years, depending on the degree of your feeble-mindedness. If you are normal people, it will take ten to twenty years. But if both of you are geniuses, it will take forty to fifty years of living together."

Ilda and I prayed, studied, planned and were determined to have a good marriage. She was four years older than I. I can honestly say this age differential never was the least handicap to a good marriage. In those days few ministers knew about premarital counselling. We were fortunate, for Drs. Harold and Blanche Miller were not only good physicians and counsellors but had become close friends. No one ever had better counselling for marriage than we did.

Finally our wedding day dawned, May 31, 1924. I had come several days earlier. Our wedding was under a towering sugar maple tree near the Bittinger home. Our families and friends stood on the grassy slopes near the tree as the sun touched the treetops on the western hills. Ezra Fike, our most trusted friend among the Maple Spring ministers, read the simple but solemn marriage ritual. And Dr. Blanche Miller and Mrs. Allie Leatherman sang wedding hymns. We were married. It was a beautiful wedding; the setting was perfect, with great trees around us and the distant ranges of the Alleghenies turning purple in the approaching dusk. Since the church did not permit church weddings, we had chosen this

50

spot as the most beautiful and meaningful to us. The tree under which the ceremony was read stood more than fifty years after that day. Not that it made the service more sacred, but it was notable for us that there were nine ministers present among the wedding guests. That should have been auspicious!

We stayed our first two nights in Ilda's home and went to Maple Spring to church on Sunday morning; the wedding was on Saturday evening. On Monday we started on our honeymoon. Her brother Foster was our chauffeur. We came that evening to the home of Esther Baer, his bride-to-be, at Lineboro, Maryland. The next evening, June 3, in a quiet service, her uncle, Noah Sellers, officiated as Foster and Esther also took their marriage vows.

The next day we drove to Hershey, Pennsylvania, and spent our honeymoon days attending the denomination's Annual Conference. A strange kind of honeymoon? Not for us. Many Brethren couples made Annual Meeting the occasion of a honeymoon, and Hershey held for us some tender and happy memories. I cannot remember much about the Conference program or business. Far more important to me was the wonder of sharing everything with the kind and gracious woman who was now my wife. I am sure we were storing up inspiration together for our years of shared ministry as a pastor-teacher couple at Onego.

On the way home, I stopped off in Keyser, West Virginia, for two days to take the West Virginia state teachers' examination. A few days later one of the men of the community at Eglon took us and our meager belongings to Onego, where we were to make our home. On the way we bought a cookstove!

By July 1, we were settled in our "parsonage." The Seneca congregation had agreed to provide a house for us, and the Mission Board would pay me $25 a month in addition to what I might earn teaching. The house they provided for us had two rooms and a lean-to kitchen. It was built of rough boards and totally innocent of paint. The last tenants had been poor housekeepers, had kept hordes of cats in the house and a brace of coon dogs under the front porch.

The environment was picturesque. The house was built on a narrow shelf of land at the foot of the north end of Spruce Mountain. In front of the house flowed a clear, boulder choked mountain stream, the Seneca. To get to the road which led to the little village of Onego, we cut down a tall sycamore tree, making it fall across the creek, elevating one end, and nailing on it rough slabs for walking and poles for a hand rail. This foot bridge was our link to the village! Twice freshets washed one end down stream, but we had the butt end of the log chained. So we would borrow Charlie Turner's horses and pull it in place again!

Women from the church had scrubbed out the little house and put flowered wallpaper in the two rooms to replace the battered Sears Roebuck catalog pages which were the only wallpaper before. Our furniture was meager but solid enough. I built book shelves of poplar boards. Our heating stove could hold several thirty-inch chunks of wood. I built a woodshed of slabs, and stocked it with red oak from a huge old tree up the mountain and sections of long-dead iron-hard locust trees. Our water supply was a spring some yards from the house, which I dug out, lined with stones, and roofed over. Farther away, I dug a pit and built a primitive outhouse. So our living quarters were two rooms, a lean-to kitchen, a woodshed, a springhouse, and a path!

There was room for a garden, and some of the church folk had already planted potatoes, corn and beans which were growing luxuriously for us when we moved in. One summer day our neighbor, Mrs. Turner, took us far up the mountainside behind our house to pick wild strawberries. Each of us brought home six or eight quarts of the most delicious, ripe, juicy berries we had ever seen. We enjoyed the mouth-watering goodness of wild strawberries all winter long.

The Roaring Plains, a segment of the 4,200-foot Allegheny Front at the head of Roaring Creek, was famous for huckleberries. Though we never went up, neighbors would go in the early morning and return late at night exhausted, with made-on-the-spot cylinder-shaped bark buckets loaded with purple juiciness of the abundant wild berries, which made gourmet quality pies. Usually they would have tales to tell of meeting bears and rattlesnakes in the berry thickets.

The first summer was a busy one! The Seneca congregation had two meeting houses. The Onego church was a half-mile from our home. It had one room and a tiny kitchen. It was set upon several big stones, so the space beneath it provided cool summertime shelter for the hogs of Clay Huffman, whose home was across the road. The other church building, called the Evergreen house, was seven miles away on the edge of the forest along the North Fork of the South Branch of the Potomac. I was expected to preach every Sunday at Onego and at least once a month at Evergreen, also at a schoolhouse on Brushy Run, four miles away, and at Timber Ridge, twelve miles away in a high valley below the massive escarpment of Spruce Mountain. We had no car, so at first I always walked or borrowed a good saddle horse for the longer journeys.

I note from my records that my first sermon as pastor was preached at Onego on June 21, on "The Meaning of the Cross." This was on a Saturday evening. The next morning Ilda and I walked to Brushy Run schoolhouse where I preached "Following Jesus." That evening I preached again at Onego. During July and August I held what we then called "revival meetings" at Onego and Brushy Run, and also began my monthly preaching services at Evergreen and Timber Ridge. From the beginning of my ministry there on June 21 to the end of December, I preached 75 sermons!

Living in this area of mountain grandeur provided us with some truly exciting recreation. On our first wedding anniversary Ilda and I climbed Spruce Knob, the highest point in West Virginia. We drove up through the fore-knobs and parked, then climbed the last 1800 feet through high pastures and a winding trail through dense alpine forest. We had learned that at the Bennet farm, far up the mountain, a good dinner could be had. Mrs. Bennet prepared a bountiful meal—country ham, fried potatoes, biscuits, and apple pie—for fifty cents each! The view of limitless forests and long deep valleys from Spruce Knob was superb. It has changed very little since then, though now a good paved road leads to the top.

Another more spectacular climb was to the top of the Seneca Rocks. I have never been a rock climber, so we took a steep trail up the shoulder of the mountain behind the rock, then eased out onto the ledges that led to the top.

Summertime found us enjoying good swimming in the deeper still pools of the Seneca near our home, and these same pools provided fair ice skating in winter.

I was appointed to teach the little one-room school at Mouth of Seneca. This was four and one-half miles from home if I took the shortcut across a small mountain spur the last mile. Of course I walked! The scenery was of surpassing grandeur. The majestic Seneca Rocks, towering 900 feet above the river, were just a half-mile from school. I had only fifteen scholars, so the teaching task was not burdensome. Furthermore, my pupils were all from good families and were eager to learn. My salary was $92 a month.

Walking to and from school was a delight during the golden fall days. At our little home there would be a good supper waiting, then I spent the evenings working on my sermons or on a correspondence course from Bethany Bible School. As winter came on we laid in a good supply of wood for heating and cooking. We found good apples ripening on two or three old trees below our house. And we picked up and stored bushels of black walnuts. I dug and roofed over a small root cellar for our potatoes, apples, and cabbages.

But we really underestimated the force of an Allegheny mountain winter! By late February our firewood was nearly exhausted. I dug out fallen locust and sycamore poles and branches and cut them up with an ax, spending several Saturdays at this job! The mountain stream froze nearly solid and the snow lay deep in the valley, while on the higher mountains nearby huge drifts built up and the dense forests of red oak and black spruce were coated with thick coats of hard, glittering frost. Often at night we could hear the deep, eerie hooting of Great Horned Owls in the trees above us on the mountain. We would bring a bucket or two of water from the spring and set them near the stove in the living room, for we could not keep the kitchen warm. At times the winter wind roared down from the Allegheny with such force that it tore the wallpaper loose from the wall of our room, forcing its way through the cracks in the rough board walls.

One January night we could scarcely keep warm in our winter blankets. The drinking water in our living room had an inch of ice on it by dawn. When I started to walk to school, though I was heavily dressed and wore a good sheepskin coat, I soon was chilled. I stopped at our little store to warm up and found the temperature was $-28°F$! Only seven of the hardier children made it to school that day.

Saturdays sometimes found us visiting the homes of parishioners. One winter day we hiked several miles up the mountain to spend the day with one of our oldest members, John Huffman. After a good dinner, Ilda and I went on higher up the mountain to the top of Mt. Porte Crayon, about 4600 feet above sea level. Here we saw dwarfed spruce trees, all their rime-coated branches growing stiffly on the east side of the trunks. The icy wind seemed to be coming from a hundred miles of Arctic mountain wastelands, and we soon headed for our warm house in the valley. The temperature was $-4°F$. at four o'clock.

The Seneca congregation was not large, and the member families were scattered over many mountain areas. The church had been started about 1856 by the missionary labors of Elder John Kline of Virginia. Two or three of our eldest members could remember the first minister of the congregation, Asa Harman, who was ordained by John Kline, and who lived across the Allegheny in Randolph County. There were several sturdy Brethren families in the area—the Vances, Adamsons, Huffmans, Mallows, Coopers, Bibles, Yocums, among them. Denominational rivalry was rather intense. The United Brethren church was perhaps stronger, with churches at Onego, North Fork and Riverton, as well as at High Rock in Germany Valley. So far as people there could remember, I was the first ordained minister of any faith actually to live in the area. The United Brethren minister lived at Riverton ten miles up the North Fork, and there were Brethren at Harman, nine miles west across the Allegheny. Nor was there any doctor nearer than fifteen miles away across the mountains.

In winter storms it was impossible to go fifteen miles away across the mountains to see our nearest doctor, and he could rarely make a house visit. Unfortunately, he often deadened his fatigue and sense of frustration with powerful infusions of homemade "corn likker." A lovely sixteen-year old neighbor, Mabel Harman, was in my eighth grade class at Onego. In mid-winter she contracted severe pneumonia. The doctor made one visit, but seemed strongly under the influence of alcohol. Two days later the girl died. Her parents were inconsolable. They had four sons, but she was their only daughter. In his desperate grief the father ordered the mother not to cry at all! He told me I could have a funeral service, but it must be very short, and there must be no music. I did the best I knew to bring God's healing mercy to them. But the mother, forced to lock her grief within her with no expression, soon ceased all communication with anyone and lived in deep depression for thirty years, until her own merciful death set her free.

The absence of resident clergy had led to some interesting social situations. Probably one third of the families were bound only to common-law marriages. When a death occurred, there were no morticians available and rarely a clergyman. A local carpenter specialized in making sturdy pine or oak coffins. Each family had its own or a shared little cemetery. The dead were laid away with a scant ceremony by the grieving family and helpful neighbors. Then in spring and summer, memorial services would be held in the churches by the itinerant ministers. This was called "preaching the funeral," and it was a time of solemnity and family reunion. Sometimes the formality of a service would be delayed until another one or more of the family had died. One Sunday, I "preached the funerals" of four members of one family—old John Huffman, his daughter, his eldest son, and a grandson—two in a morning service, and after a bountiful basket dinner, the sermon for the son and grandson in the afternoon service.

A story was told there of a man whose wife died in early winter, leaving him with several small children. Before a minister could preach her funeral the next summer, the man had quite happily taken a new wife. Then when the first wife's funeral was preached, the good man sobbed on the shoulder of his second wife. After the sermon, the minister performed the belated marriage service for them, too!

In February of our first year, I was asked to come to Riverton, ten miles from home, to be principal and seventh and eighth grade teacher in the four-room school there. I accepted, and Ilda took over the school at Mouth of Seneca. She boarded in a good home near the school Monday through Thursday, and I too found a room and board in Riverton. We would walk to our school communities on Sunday evening or Monday morning, and after five days of teaching would meet at Harper's store, near her school, and walk home together. It was strenuous but now we had a fabulous income! Ilda's salary was larger than mine, and soon we felt we could afford a car! We bought a used Model T Ford roadster—a good car which really was a blessing to us. It cost us $300 and served us five years. Our nearest graded road was the one from Franklin to Petersburg, twenty-seven miles away either across the dangerous North Fork mountain or down the winding road through the gap to Petersburg.

Ilda's brother, Foster, and his wife, Esther, were in a home mission church at Jordan Run, twenty-five miles down the North Fork from us. He also taught school and had three preaching places. They lived in a comfortable old log cabin in the mountain hollow a mile from their church. Twice in the first year we visited them. The first time, before my first school term began, we walked about twenty-five miles! Then soon after we bought our car, we decided to drive to see them. We left home in late afternoon on April 3. The Seneca was swollen from melting snow in the mountains. When we attempted to ford it at Mouth of Seneca, we got stuck among the polished river rocks, in three feet of icy water. I waded out and got a neighbor with a truck to push us on through. The road the next fifteen miles was nothing but deep muddy ruts. Finally, about four miles from their home, we got to a stretch of fairly solid road, only to have a back wheel come off!

We abandoned the car — it was nine at night now — and walked the rest of the way in pitch darkness! The next morning Foster and I walked down to the car, put the wheel back on, and finally got it to his home. That day was beautiful, and we decided to hike to the top of the Allegheny Front, and to Stony River Dam, a few miles away. We drove our cars (Foster also had a small Ford) as far as we could, then climbed for an hour. At the top there was no trail, so we struck off through the stunted spruce trees and granite boulders in what we thought was the right direction. We were dismayed when suddenly it was sunset and we could not find our way back. We found the ruins of an old lumber camp. We had brought a little picnic supper which we ate, then built a huge fire of old timbers and tried our best to keep warm. There was little sleep! In the morning the ground was frozen hard a few yards from our fire. We found bobcat tracks in a soft place only a few feet away. As the morning mists lifted around us we could hear the deep booming drumming of ruffed grouse cocks. As soon as it was light, we found our way back to our cars and just had time for a hot breakfast before church. Foster had asked me to preach. He and our wives all had a losing battle with sleep while I preached! That evening I preached in our Evergreen church, and so home to bed!

To return to my story! On August 4, 1924, I began my first big "revival meeting" at the Brushy Run schoolhouse. A revival was a big event in those remote communities. There were no radios, televisions, movies or dances, so the revival meeting was a big social occasion, the only exciting event, and everybody came! All that first day, Ilda and I visited in homes, some of them far up the mountain slopes. At evening, the crowd gathered; most people walked, some came on horseback. They brought their babies, their coon dogs, their snuff cans, and some their rifles and jugs of moonshine "likker!" Soon the little building was packed and many were standing outside. I preached as well as I knew how, but I'm sure it wasn't adequate. The people wanted more lurid threats of hell fire, more juicy denunciation of sin than I knew how to deliver.

After the service was over, Deacon Ike Mallow came to me and said, "Now we are fixin' to have you stay with us tonight. It ain't a fur piece up the Run. If'n your woman is tired she can ride my old mare — you and Owen (his grown son) and me can walk." Of course we accepted his invitation, though Ilda didn't try to ride the old mare — no saddle! As we walked up the narrow stony path beside Brushy Run, one family after another said goodnight and stopped at their log cabins. The last mile up the flank of Spruce Mountain was through dark virgin forest of tall hemlock trees. There was no road, only a trail.

When we finally arrived, he ushered us into his one-room cabin. At one end of the room there were two beds and a trundle bed, laden with three or four little children. Mrs. Mallow got up from one bed, her three bigger daughters from another. We were completely exhausted, and wondered where we would sleep! A ladder led up through what seemed a loft floor of rough poles. After some sleepy talk, the mother spread a dark blanket where she had been lying, the big girls climbed the ladder with Owen to some pallets on the loft floor, and she said kindly, "Now Brother, you and your woman can lay down on that bed!" Ike and his wife took the bed the girls had been sleeping on. We weren't sure how much undressing we should do. Finally Ilda slipped off shoes and dress, and I my shoes and shirt and tie, and we went to bed! There was no mattress nor sheets, only two rather grimy blankets on hard planks! About the time our host began some ferocious snoring, Ilda began to squirm and slap—an army of fleas and bed bugs had rushed to repel the invaders. We slept little! And when the first faint dawn light came through the one window of the cabin, we were all ready to rise and shine! Insect bites do not affect me, but Ilda was a mass of welts and swellings.

Soon Mrs. Mallow had a bountiful breakfast ready—freshly baked biscuits with fresh butter and honey from wild bees; thick slabs of bacon; all the fried eggs we could eat; and big thick cups of welcome strong black coffee laced with chicory! The Mallows begged us to stay all day, and we did! Their cabin was the last up that valley. Beyond was mile after mile of dense forest, and beyond the head of Brushy Run was the top of Spruce Knob, the highest point in the state.

Later in the day Ilda and I followed a clear cold mountain stream far up into the forest. It was teaming with rainbow trout. After a while we found a deep, clear, shaded pool, and both of us stripped and had a good swim in the cold mountain water. The pool was so full of trout that they bumped into us and nibbled at our toes!

We spent two weeks in this valley, usually walking to a different home each night. In some of the homes we had delicious meals; in others, we had to close our eyes to flies baked into biscuits, water glasses so grimy one could not see the water, and dogs and chickens under the table! But all these were our people! They offered us the best they had, and they were so hungry for the kind of spiritual food they thought I could offer them. How I wished I could really satisfy that hunger.

In our second summer I again held several revival meetings. The one at Evergreen was especially memorable. A mile or two down the river there was a family with several grown sons who were notorious moonshiners and who regularly went on great sprees, terrorizing their neighbors and upsetting the whole community. In the summer of 1922, Ilda's cousin Lester Fike spent the summer months in the area, holding evangelistic meetings. When he preached at Evergreen, the moonshining boys and their pals shot through the open windows and splintered the chimneys of some of the kerosene lamps. Another night they set off dynamite, tying the sticks to a tree outside the church!

When I started holding a revival then, in August 1925, these characters boasted that they would soon put a stop to it! The first night, while I was preaching, they backed their car to the door of the church, opened the throttle, and to that accompaniment they stalked down the aisle, hats on, cigarettes dangling, big revolvers on their hips, and spitting tobacco juice on the floor. Soon they left, and we continued the service. The community people were scared and indignant, and they invited the local law officer, Constable Harley Vance, to come with me the next evening to keep order. Harley hid among the trees as the service began. Only a handful of people were present. Soon after the service began we heard a big explosion, evidently a mile or more away; then everything was quiet.

The constable and I were to stay that night in the home of Ben Cooper, a deacon who lived near the church — and near the moonshiners. As we approached the Cooper home we were stopped by a drunken man with a rifle, one of the gang. Explaining to the constable, he said, "We were on the way to church, but we drove off the road. There sure would have been hell if we got there!" The constable had warrants to arrest these fellows for disturbing worship the evening before. He deputized the Cooper sons, Ernie and Ped, and me, to go with him to find the others. We found four more, all rousing drunk, all armed. Then we found their car, wrecked against a tree. In it we found some rope, a pile of rocks, a half case of dynamite and boxes of rifle and shotgun cartridges. Hell at the church indeed! The fellows, all of them of the gang who had disturbed the service the previous night, were served warrants and a few days later appeared before the local justice of the peace. He quickly announced that this was a serious offence, and that they must be tried in the county court at Franklin. I was never summoned to testify, but the rumor soon spread that the moonshiners had given the state's attorney a keg of choice corn "likker," and he dropped all charges against them.

This isn't quite the end of the story. A few weeks later these men broke into the Evergreen church, tore up hymnals and the Bible and burned the church to the ground. They also freely let it be known that if "that damn preacher" ever dared to come down the North Fork again, they would shoot him! The United Brethren minister offered me the use of his church after ours was burned, and we gladly accepted his hospitality. I had some fear of the outlaws' threats, and though I kept going for my regular monthly service, I did not tell my wife of the threats!

There were many wonderful people in this mountain area; most were frugal, sturdy folk, with deep roots in the land, and with high standards of conduct. One man whom I admired greatly had two thousand acres of fine mountain grazing land and kept thousands of prize-winning sheep and many cattle. He was college-trained, and while riding miles caring for his sheep he would pass the time reciting the great English poets' choicest works! His brother also was cultured and gracious. They and their families, though not Brethren, frequently attended our services and were most hospitable and gracious. These, the Walter and Milton Dolly families, we counted as wonderfully kind friends.

I had little training for ministry and I am sure I made many mistakes. My preaching was too dogmatic and I did not know how to be a pastor to my people. Shortly before leaving home, my Uncle Sam Ziegler was visiting in our home. He quizzed me about my plans, approved my approaching marriage, then said coolly, "I don't think any preacher has much to say that's helpful before he's thirty!" I was shocked and perhaps a bit hurt. I determined I would prove him wrong. But with the little preparation for ministry I had, perhaps he was all too right, at least in my first two years as a pastor! It took a lot of courage, even bravado, to try it!

Yet many of our people were kind in their responses. Up until then they had services only monthly or less, except for an occasional summer revival and an annual Love Feast. The visiting ministers were usually some of the free ministers from Maple Spring, in Preston County.

I had my first baptisms, weddings, and funerals in my two years at Onego. I baptized ten young people in a deep clear pool in Seneca Creek, right beside the church. The first person I baptized, an eighteen year old girl named Iva Harper, also figured in one of my first weddings. She was an orphan girl, who lived here and there in homes in the community as a hired girl. For some months she stayed in a home far up on the Allegheny, where the mother was sickly and Iva did all the housework. Often she came down to church, bringing the oldest boy Elmer, who was about eighteen. One day she came to our home, smiling, and said to me, "Brother Z, if'n you're going to be home tomorrow, I'm a'going to fetch Elmer with me, and we want you to hitch us!" I agreed, and the next morning they came, Elmer with the first clean new overalls I had ever seen him wear. With them came the kindly neighbor, Floyd Huffman, who was her unofficial guardian. When they stood before me in our little living room, I was about to say, "Let us pray," when suddenly Iva turned to Mr. Huffman and exclaimed, "Darn your hide, Floyd, if you laugh, I'll bust your head!" Then I solemnly went on with service.

On the evening of January 2, 1926, a bitter cold night, Ilda had invited a dozen of the younger people of the community in for a surprise birthday party. Soon after they had gone—about nine o'clock—there was a timid knock on our door. There stood a man, thirtyish, from far up Roaring Creek, and a woman with him. I invited them in. They were shivering with cold, for they had been waiting outside in the snow for nearly an hour until our guests had gone. When we got them thawed out and plied them with coffee and leftover birthday cake, the man explained that they had come to be married. They had the license, and after some conversation they stood before me as I read the marriage service. Then soon they left happily, hand in hand, to walk five miles back up the creek to their home and their four children! Roscoe was a tenant farmer. He had just been employed by one of the good landowners who told him, "I'm glad to have you work my farm and live on it, but you must get properly married!"

The second year we lived there I taught grades five through eight in the two-room school just a quarter mile from home. Ilda did not teach that year. We had thought she would probably have our first child that fall, but to our sorrow no baby was on the way!

As our second year drew to a close, we planned to move to Bridgewater, where I would go to college; perhaps both of us could complete college. Bridgewater was the church college for that area, and we had learned to know some fine church leaders who were Bridgewater College graduates. Ilda's brother Foster had one more year to complete his course, so we planned to share a rented house in the town of Bridgewater.

We left Onego early in June with our few possessions, our little Model T Ford, and about $500 in savings, in time for Foster and me to take several summer school courses. I thought then I would not go on in the ministry. The work had been hard, the visible results were few. I had loved my five years as a schoolmaster, and planned to prepare for a career in teaching. Yet it was hard to say good-bye to a dozen families who had not only been patient with a very inexperienced preacher, but had become very warm friends. I believe Ilda's kind, patient, quiet manner and her selfless work in church, vacation school, and in the community kept the two years from being an entire failure.

CHAPTER 5

Preparing for Ministry

Early in June 1926, Ilda and I arrived in Bridgewater. The rolling hills and rich farmlands and the misty blue of the mountain ranges on either side of the Shenandoah Valley made the setting of the sleepy little college town seem spacious and idyllic after our two years among the steep, rugged West Virginia mountains. Foster and Esther and we moved our scanty furnishings into a square frame house beside the North River Bridge, a mile from the college. Bridgewater was then a very small college with two hundred students, most of them Brethren. There were five small brick buildings containing the college dining room and kitchen. The Bridgewater Church, right on the edge of the campus, seemed very imposing, after having been where the frame meeting houses were of one small room set on rocks!

We spent three good, busy, exciting years in Bridgewater. I entered as a freshman, though I felt out of place and quite superior to most of my class who were four or five years younger and just out of high school. By enrolling in two summer terms and taking a heavy course load, I was able to graduate in three years, in 1929. I expected college courses to be easy, for had I not already had five years' experience teaching and preaching?

Early in the year I had a rude shock. Though I saw little need for it, I was required to take Freshman English. The instructor, a smart, attractive young woman just two years older then I, also taught history. Very soon she assigned to each student the writing of a paper. I breezed through the writing, typed my essay hastily and carelessly, and turned it in, expecting at least an A + . To my consternation, Miss Kurtz handed my paper back the next period with the words "Insufferably Dull!" in huge letters scrawled clear down the first page! That shock was greatly needed! I am sure I must have seemed a pompous egoist to her and perhaps to other professors and students as well. I swallowed my pride and went to work. This same young professor turned me on in the study of history. To her I owe a rude but stimulating awakening.

Through the first year, I was unsure about the future. But about April President Paul Bowman, whom I greatly admired, called me to his office. We talked at some length and he gave me strong encouragement not to forsake the ministry, but to plan for full college and graduate training for it. The occasional sermons and chapel talks I heard him give, the warmth of his personal interest in me, helped to turn me again to what I am sure was God's unshaken purpose for me. Another factor in my renewed interest in ministry was the eloquent preaching of the young Bridgewater pastor, M. Guy West. I joined the Clericus, the student ministers' association, and also became a member of Professor Nelson Huffman's College Glee Club. I became involved in quite a few deputation trips to churches and had frequent invitations to preach.

Ilda was employed by the Bridgewater School to teach a kindergarten class, which she did for two school years. Dr. Bowman one day asked me whether I would consider a summer pastorate at Manassas, Virginia. With some misgivings, I accepted. Since we desperately needed money, Ilda spent the summer of 1927 teaching Vacation Bible Schools in West Virginia, and I went on alone to Manassas.

The summer pastorate was the real crisis point in my choice of direction. I found myself in a strong rural church, with good families and a warm, eager response to my preaching and teaching. I stayed in various homes a week at a time, visited every home in the congregation, held revival meetings at both the Cannon Branch meeting house and the small church at Bradley, and taught in vacation schools at both places.

The older ministers, E. E. Blough and J. M. Kline, were most cordial and helpful to me. Here I was among many cousins—the Conners, Harleys and Bloughs, though I had never known them before. The kindness and response of this congregation was so overwhelming that never again in all my life have I wanted to turn away from my calling to preach! During that summer, more than twenty persons made their choice to follow Christ, and were baptized in beautiful Broad Run below E. E. Blough's farm. Incidentally, I was the first paid pastor the church had; and forty-eight years later, I returned to serve nine months as interim pastor of the church.

Foster Bittinger graduated in 1927 and moved to a pastorate at Browntown, some fifty miles down the Shenandoah Valley. Ilda and I moved closer to the campus, and became quite involved in college life. As I look back on my education at Bridgewater, I recall with deep gratitude some of the professors who most influenced me. I have already mentioned Ada Kurtz, whose sharp criticism gave me a swift kick toward real work in writing. Dr. John S. Flory, the kind, scholarly former president, taught English Literature and a course in Old Testament which really opened my mind to see the glory of our literary and biblical heritage! Allen Bicknell's teaching of German, his droll stories, and his delight in singing "Dick Deadeye" in H. M. S. Pinafore, endeared him to many of us. One day in German Literature class, we were reading and translating *Flachsmann als Erzieher*, when my friend, Earnest Muntzing, came on the expression, "fett and feissig." He soberly translated it "corpulent and pusillanimous!" Dr. Bicknell laughed so heartily that he could scarcely continue teaching!

I found the sciences fascinating — the rigorous discipline of math with Professor C. E. Shull and the wonders of biology with Professor Edward Van Pelt. In my senior year, I was assistant in botany, with special assignment to collect plants for the Virginia Herbarium. I found and identified one wild flower which had never before been identified in Virginia. Field trips in the beautiful mountains around us were a joy. In addition I taught a class in algebra that year. Several of my classmates who had flunked algebra as freshmen and had to have it for graduation enrolled in my class. This presented quite a dilemma! To flunk any of them meant he could not graduate. And I could not bring myself to give a grade a student did not deserve! I never tried harder to do good teaching; I was able in all good faith to give all five of my senior classmates passing grades!

In the summer of 1928, I took a few courses in the summer term and spent most of my time as summer pastor of the Barren Ridge Church of the Brethren near Staunton. Also, I continued to preach often throughout the three years and held two or three revival meetings. One of these was particularly strenuous. It was at the Greene County Industrial School, the ambitious home mission boarding and day school project which the General Mission Board had established for the primitive people in the eastern slopes of the Blue Ridge Mountains. A remarkable and courageous little woman, Miss Nelie Wampler, had devoted her whole life to these mountain people. A strong team of highly trained and dedicated young couples conducted the school, which offered the only secondary education in the county.

The church there had meeting places in several coves — Shifflet Hollow, Mutton Hollow, Beacon Hallow, Shiloh — and at the school. I spent a busy nine days there, preaching every evening to students and community people who came in good numbers. Every morning after breakfast with the school children, Principal Orville Hersch would draw me a map, give me a saddle horse, and start me out on a round of visiting families in the community. I would return in late evening, tired, hungry and saddlesore! But the mountain people were hospitable and the response was good. Some fifteen persons made their decisions for Christ during the meetings. I have no record of my preaching appointments for one six-month period while in college, but the records I do have show nearly two hundred sermons preached during these three years.

Though I enjoyed public speaking, for some reason I did not get into debating during my college years. But I did represent Bridgewater in the peace oratorical contests among Brethren colleges each of my three years—and each time placed second! Also, I represented Bridgewater in a state collegiate oratorical contest. I suspect the judges in this latter contest were not favorably impressed by my impassioned speech against all wars!

A significant branch of the student Christian movement was the Student Volunteer Movement for Foreign Missions. This organization had been founded by the veteran ecumenist John R. Mott, and had enormous effect in challenging many of the most idealistic university and college students to prepare for foreign missionary service. Ilda and I were members of our campus branch of the movement. There was a state organization, of which I became vice president. At an annual state convention at William and Mary College, I met a young missionary to the Philippine Islands named Frank Laubach, with whom I later had a deep and important friendship.

A Church of the Brethren branch of the Student Volunteer Movement provided a steady stream of strong candidates for the expanding missionary program of the church, in India, China, and Africa. I served two years as president of this organization. While Bridgewater had most of its foreign missionary alumni serving in China, our own interests were most deeply in India, and we hoped that ultimately our career would be there. The Student Volunteer organization on the Bridgewater College campus was very active in cooperation with the Clericus in sending out deputation teams to the churches all across the region. I had the privilege of attending two of the quadrennial conventions of the International Student Volunteer Movement, one in Detroit in 1928, the other in Toronto in 1940 when I represented Bethany Theological Seminary.

Because of my age and being already married, my ties with fellow students were not as strong as I could have desired. Yet they were deep and abiding friendships with a number of persons and ministers. Among them were Raymond Peters, Samuel Harley, Carson Key, A. Ray Showalter, Guy Wampler, M. Guy West and his wife, Naomi Miller West, Douglas Nininger, Cecil Ikenberry, and DeWitt L. Miller.

Deputation trips developed our skills in speaking, and I think helped to interest local churches in the missionary outreach of the church. The trips were also times of good comradeship! One such occasion provided an adventure which is still a source of reminiscent chuckles for all of us involved. Four of us who were student ministers—Clarence Bowman, J. Curtis Miller, Edwin Shoemaker and I—were on our way to Tennessee for a crowded Easter weekend of meetings. Driving through Southwest Virginia on a very narrow road, we were slowed down for miles by an ancient farm truck, which stayed firmly in the middle of the road. Finally Miller, who was driving, passed the truck, but slipping a bit on the wet clay shoulders, he nipped the truck's front bumper. The truck driver blew his horn furiously and tried to follow us. Soon we left him behind. Some miles further on, as we approached Bristol, we came upon a formidable road block by six policemen. They surrounded our car, asked if any of us were from West Virginia. Miller readily admitted that he was. The police informed us that a message from Abingdon, fifteen miles back, had alerted them that we had forced a truck off the road and were a gang of criminals wanted for murder in West Virginia! We tried to explain who we really were and what had happened, but the officers insisted on taking us to police headquarters in Bristol. One officer bravely got in the car with us, and we were escorted by five others in a cavalcade of cars and motorcycles!

By the time we arrived the officer who rode with us was convinced that we were not criminals and told the others, "Boys, we've been had; we've brought in a bunch of preachers!" The desk officer called Abingdon to have the informant come to Bristol, but he had fled! The police were embarrassed, and very cordial to us. As we left, one said, "Please don't tell anyone in Bristol what happened — we'd never hear the last of it!"

One of the happy memories of our three years at Bridgewater surrounds our lasting friendship with people of the community. Ilda's work as kindergarten teacher, my good summer days working for various farmers in the community, and our involvements in teaching in the Bridgewater Sunday School were refreshing and were happily remembered when eighteen years later I was called to the pastorate of the Bridgewater Church.

As the final year drew to its close, we were naturally concerned for the future. We were not ready for foreign service and could not afford going right on to Seminary. Again Dr. Paul Bowman was helpful. He arranged for us to visit the flourishing young church in Johnson City, Tennessee. Established only two years earlier, and with a stately and functional building, the place seemed very attractive. The call of the church seemed to us to corroborate the leading of God in the matter. We accepted, and soon after graduation we moved to Tennessee, to my first full-time pastorate.

While Johnson City was a new congregation, it had its roots in a strong historic Brethren community in Washington County. Paul Bowman's home church was Knob Creek, only three miles away. The first religious service ever held in Johnson City was held by Elder Jack Pence, a Brethren minister. Now the congregation had its modern church building on Chilhowie Avenue, in a clean beautiful city of 25,000. There were about two hundred members in the church when we came.

During the two years there, I preached in two services each Sunday and both of us helped in Sunday School. We initiated a program of visitation evangelism which was quite successful. While I have lost some of my records, we probably received fifty persons into the church in two years. On Easter evening, 1931, I baptized twenty-seven, many of them adults. One young married woman who was baptized called me late that night to tell me that her husband was much upset. He wanted to be baptized, too, but in the river. She had gone ahead without him, and now he refused to be baptized at all. I visited them the next day and we worked out a compromise: he would be baptized if she would, too, in the river. I assured her that this would not repudiate her baptism in the church, and she gladly offered this compromise so he would come, too. So the next evening a group of us drove out to a quiet place along the Watauga River, and I baptized the couple in the still icy waters of the river!

I immediately became involved there in the activities of the Tennessee District. Within a year, the District Ministerial Board recommended ordination to the eldership; and on September 30, 1930, I was ordained by Sam Garst, who was our moderator, and William H. Swadley, a gracious banker-preacher who was a steadfast leader in our local church. By this time I had developed a keen interest in worship and music and held a few institutes in churches of the district seeking to develop this aspect of church life.

This young church had strong leadership and great potential for growth. One couple who gave us strong support was John Bowman White and his wife, Amy Trout White. They lived fifteen miles away at Sulphur Springs where John was the high school principal. When we had been there a year, the Whites moved to Nashville. John was doing graduate work, and Amy taught high school mathematics. Their wise counsel and close friendship were a great source of strength to us. William and Laura Swadley likewise were close and dependable support. Laura, a brilliant Bible teacher, had been a professor in Bethany Bible School before marrying and coming to Tennessee. Several Bowman families also were faithful and resourceful members of the fellowship.

One unhappy division in the church occured while I was pastor there. A popular preacher in the area was Elder A.M. Laughrun, a fiery camp-meeting type of revivalist. Four of his sisters and their families were members of our congregation. Elder Laughrun wrote to inform us that he wished to come to Johnson City and hold a revival meeting in which he proposed to preach every night on the Second Coming of Christ. Our church board gave the matter much prayerful consideration, and we informed Brother Laughrun that his proposal did not fit into our church program and that we could not invite him to come at that time. Laughrun considered this a serious affront and raised quite a furor about the matter among his family and friends. One result was the withdrawal of all his relatives and a few others from the church!

Ilda had a great interest in the Christian nurture of children and became one of the first district directors of children's work in the Church of the Brethren. She became an expert in vacation Bible schools. Together we conducted a week's camp for junior children at a scenic spot beside the Watauga River near the city. We also organized a Boy Scout troop, of which I was the first scoutmaster.

An event of personal importance to us during the Johnson City days was the arrival of our son Robert. After five years of marriage, there seemed little hope of our having a child of our own. So we planned to adopt a baby. We found a month-old bright-eyed baby boy in a highly recommended child shelter in Knoxville, Tennessee. Shortly before Christmas in 1929 we brought him to our home, and in due course adopted him. Though not our biological son, I can say after nearly fifty years that there has never been a single moment of regret or alienation in our relationship.

In January 1931, Charles D. Bonsack, secretary of the General Mission Board of the Church of the Brethren, and a long time counsellor and friend, wrote to ask whether we would be willing to go that year as missionaries to India. Our work in Johnson City was so rewarding that we really had to re-examine our goals and pray for God's guidance. It soon became clear that this was the road on which God had been leading us and that we should accept this call. While our people in the church assured us they would like for us to stay, they were supportive of our call and felt pride in having their pastor family chosen to go as missionaries. There was a certain glamour and excitement still extant then in the church about foreign missions, a glow that in a few more years with the vast changes in church and world led to a rapid eclipse of missionary spirit.

I acquired my graduate theological training in an unfortunately piecemeal fashion. Before entering Bridgewater I had taken several helpful correspondence courses from Bethany Bible School. When we were called to go to India, though I felt keenly the lack of adequate training, Brother Bonsack assured me that I could use an extended furlough time to complete my seminary education.

While in the Johnson City pastorate, the opportunity came to attend intensive seminars for rural pastors, at Vanderbilt University. Being a home mission pastor made me eligible for this special training. Ten or twelve Brethren pastors shared these seminars with several hundred ministers from across the nation. In one of these seminars we heard John R. Mott, the noted mission statesman, give a remarkable series of lectures on the ministry of laymen.

We stayed seven and one half years in India, so when I entered resident study on the Bethany campus in the fall of 1939 I was thirty-six years old and had had a wealth of experience. We stayed at Bethany the full year and also the summer term of four weeks. By taking twenty hours of class work it was possible to complete half of my three years' course by July 1940. Studying the Bible with W. W. Slabaugh, Church History under Floyd Mallott, Theology with William Beahm, Psychology with Perry Rohrer, and Devotional Practices and New Testament Studies with the saintly A. C. Wieand, were rich learning experiences.

Instead of taking another year of furlough to finish my seminary work, we had to change our life plans quite drastically. Because Ilda had become a brittle diabetic, we were advised not to return to India for health reasons. It then seemed best to go at once into full-time work in the home church and to finish the seminary work in small segments. Confronted by two invitations to service, one to be executive secretary for the Southeastern Region of the church, the other to become the pastor of a large congregation in York, Pennsylvania, we felt strongly guided to the pastorate. More of this experience later.

After five years in York, I was invited by President V. F. Schwalm to teach Bible and Christian Education at Manchester College. We moved to Manchester for the beginning of the college year in 1945. Since it was deemed essential to have a graduate degree for college teaching, I asked leave for the spring quarter and returned to Bethany. Here and at Chicago Theological Seminary for spring terms and Garrett for the summer, I completed most of the work for the seminary degree in this way.

During the next busy year of teaching at Manchester, I carried on independent study under the direction of Bethany professors and received the Bachelor of Divinity degree at the 1947 Bethany commencement. A book on worship which I had written and published in India was accepted as the required dissertation for graduation. Thus ended the formal, resident part of my education. But today, at seventy-five, it seems that vast horizons of knowledge and wisdom still stretch on ahead. God grant that my education may never be completed!

CHAPTER 6

We Purchase Pith Helmets

After leaving Johnson City, I spent the summer of 1931 in evangelistic meetings at Brownsville, Maryland; Lebanon, Pennsylvania; Manassas, Virginia; and the Fairview Church at Cordova, Maryland. We had driven to Colorado Springs for the Annual Conference. At this conference we were interviewed by the General Mission Board and approved. Then we were presented with several other candidates in the missionary convocation and consecrated with the impressive ceremony of laying on of hands. The consecration prayer was offered by S. Z. Sharp, the noble old educator who had founded the first Brethren school for higher education and who was ninety-five years old. His prayer was offered in stately and reverent language and was a marvelous benediction to us who were just at the threshold of our larger service in the church.

During the crowded summer months, Ilda spent much time at the homes of her parents and mine, preparing for our journey. In addition to the evangelistic meetings, I preached at several other churches, the last sermon in the Lebanon Church in Pennsylvania, the church which undertook my support as a missionary.

We left home on September 23, 1931, for New York. There we were met by Brother Bonsack, our foreign mission secretary, and our travelling companions, I. W. and Mabel Moomaw and their two sons David and Richard, who were returning to India after their first furlough; Anna Warstler, a teacher and religious educator; and Ruth Glessner and Hazel Messer, registered nurses. We sailed from New York to London on a slow old Cunard liner, the *Caronia*. Five glorious days were spent in London, then we crossed England by train to Liverpool, where we embarked in a small steamer, the *Elysia,* for the leisurely journey to India. In all, we spent five weeks in travel, getting acquainted with our fellow missionaries and enjoying all the delightful pursuits of life on a slow boat to Asia. Our Robert had just passed his second birthday and soon had the run of the ship. He seemed to meet all new challenges of the trip with great zest. Our only stop between Liverpool and Bombay was at Port Said, where we purchased our pith helmets which were then considered absolute necessities for northerners in tropical India or Africa. Many sights along the way filled us with wonder and sometimes awe — the great rock of Gibraltar as we entered the deep blue waters of the Mediterranean Sea, the Suez Canal, the desolate grandeur of Mt. Sinai off to the east as we sailed south toward the Red Sea. Then early one morning we were awakened by landing preparations on deck. We hurried out and saw the long broken line of the Western Ghat mountains blue in the dawn as we steamed into the vast harbor of Bombay on Sunday, November 1.

Soon we stepped on shore, greeted by several missionaries who had come down from Gujarat, two hundred miles northward, to meet the newcomers. A few hours later, after the bewildering drive in an open carriage from the dock to the railway station through the incredibly crowded bazaar streets, we were deposited with our baggage and our new friends in a third-class railway carriage with board benches and dusty floors, for the ten-hour journey to Anklesvar, our first home in India. The rail journey was intensely interesting. The railroad follows the Arabian Sea coast, with foothills and mountains to the east. Since Anklesvar was our farthest north mission station, we met missionaries and Indian Christians at other stations — Palghar, Dahanu Road, Bulsar and Jalalpur — as we travelled slowly northward. A great treat was an abundance of small, delicious, green-skinned bananas, which we bought from station hucksters for four cents a dozen! Other fruit merchants sold us mangoes and dates.

At eleven p.m. we left the train and were welcomed by a large crowd of smiling, brown-skinned Indian Christians and several missionaries. Soon we were at the home of the D. J. Lichtys, a spacious, cool bungalow with wide verandas, where we were to be at home for our first year of intensive language study. All of our party except Hazel Messer came this far. The Moomaws returned to their pleasant house just yards from the Lichty home. The other two ladies were to live at the Girls' Practical Arts School campus a mile away.

The Lichtys soon seemed like parents to us. "Uncle Dan" Lichty had come to India as a rural missionary in 1902, the year before I was born! His wife, Anna, was a charming, gracious hostess who made us feel at home at once. By midnight we were ready to settle down under our mosquito nets for our first night in India. This was the most pleasant time of the year in India. The rains were over and the clear air had turned cool. All around us many kinds of crops were ripening, most of them new to us. It seemed that stars had never been so brilliant, the sky never so velvety black as on these first Indian nights.

We were awakened at dawn by the hearty singing of the boys and young men in their morning chapel service a hundred yards away in the Rhoades Memorial Training School building. Here a hundred or so village boys and young men were getting superb training to go back to their rural areas as farmers, carpenters and teachers.

At seven the first morning, the headmaster of the training college, Premchand G. Bhagat, came to the house to give us our first lesson in the Gujarati language. I have never known a more brilliant teacher! Whether working with us on the language, teaching classes in education to the young men, preaching or expounding a Bible lesson to adults in church, he was always stimulating, demanding, leading, prodding, encouraging. The Anklesvar Training College achieved the reputation of being one of the two or three best such institutions in all India, through his leadership and the constructive and creative support of I. W. Moomaw and A. F. Bollinger.

Our first year was an intensive learning experience, with many hours a day in language study and many hours spent with people — visiting the villages with the Lichtys, learning to talk with the courteous high spirited students and teachers in the training school, and worshipping in the big, airy Anklesvar Church a half-mile away. One of our language teachers was a young Hindu from the town near by. He knew little English, but was a purist in his love for and use of his own language. Always dressed in spotless white homespun, he was soon the ideal Hindu to us.

One one side of our homes was a row of small comfortable houses where the teachers lived; on the other was a small village of Moslem farmers. Often we were awakened at dawn by the high tenor chant of the *muezzin* calling the faithful men to prayer in the little mosque before they had their morning tea and were off to the day's work in the fields.

The boys in the Vocational Training School were not only learning to be good carpenters, teachers and farmers. They also spent several hours a day in the gardens and fields, working in the carpenter shop with master carpenter Bikaji, or with the chickens, learning from Botilal. The agriculture teacher was a resourceful young Hindu named Shanabhai, who had an uncanny ability to pass on his love for the land to students who had really hoped to escape into some white collar job. A major goal of this school was to see the young men go back eagerly to the villages as resourceful, dedicated Christian leaders prepared to lift the quality of rural life on every level, economic, spiritual and intellectual. That almost all of the boys did go back with this spirit, and usually became leaders of the church and community, demonstrated the success of this ideal. The girls in the Practical Arts School were inspired with the same lofty ideals.

We had no motor cars in our mission stations, no electric power, no running water in our homes and, to our amazement, no screens! Transportation was by ox-carriages, bicycles, walking, and between stations by railway trains which were frequent, if slow, and very cheap. It was a standing joke that only fools and Englishmen travelled first class; Parsees and wealthy people rode second class; and missionaries travelled third class because there was no fourth! Third class carriages had wooden benches facing each other, upper shelves for baggage or sleeping, and doors at the ends of each compartment. For long journeys or inter-station visiting we always carried bedding rolls, which could be opened up—if there was room—for overnight train journeys. Train journeys gave opportunity for lively conversation with all kinds of common folk, who asked us many questions—"Who are you? What do you missionaries do? What salary do you get?" We were always evasive in answering the salary question, for even our meager subsistance wage seemed a pricely sum to Indian peasants. So we answered, usually to their satisfaction, "khawanu-pivanu," which meant our food and drink. Knowing British habits, I suspect that many believed we were supplied with beef and plenty of liquor!

Our lifestyle was simple, for we wanted to live as nearly on the level of our neighbors as was consistent with maintaining our health in a rather hostile tropical climate. We ate no beef at all, for this would be most repugnant to our Hindu neighbors even if it were available; and no pork, for the only meat merchants were Moslems, and they abhor pigs. So our proteins came from occasional goat meat, fish, and poultry, also milk and peanuts. The milk we used was from water buffaloes. It was high (seven percent) in rather indigestible butter fat. It had to be boiled, and the clotted cream with fruit preserves or syrup on toast was a breakfast treat. We ate a great deal of rice, lentils, and vegetables. Delicious fruits —bananas, mangoes, papayas, guavas, and custard apples—were abundant and cheap. So we were never under-nourished! Because all the missionary women were assigned tasks in the mission program and shopping in the bazaars for food was time consuming and tricky, each missionary family employed a cook, usually a man, who was an expert in shopping, and often an accomplished chef!

Our houses were large and surrounded by cool verandas. During the summer—February to June—the dry heat at most of our stations was not too hard to endure, until temperatures would soar over 110° nearly every day for weeks. We found that our missionaries had learned most of their living habits from the Irish Presbyterian missionaries who were our nearest mission neighbors and who had brought their traditional British customs to India with them. Since they did not use screens, we did not either. But screens or no, it was imperative to sleep under big nets to ward off the malaria-bearing Anopheles mosquitoes.

We spent fifteen months at Anklesvar. Our first duty was to learn the Gujarati language and to get acquainted with the Indian people. I found the learning of the beautiful Gujarati language and literature very pleasant and rather easy. Ilda always found a new language quite difficult, and though she worked hard at it, she never was proficient in it. Bobby, our two-year-old, was chattering colloquial Gujarati within weeks with his coterie of little Indian friends. Learning English and Gujarati side by side, he never mixed the languages, as we adults tended to do.

I preached my first sermon in India at Vali, two weeks after our arrival, through the pastor's translation, though I did read my text in Gujarati. I used this method in preaching for the first six months. My first sermon in Gujarati was in June, 1932, and from that time I also taught a daily Bible class in the Vocational Training School.

Because of the rigors of the climate, our missionaries, especially those with school-aged children, took six-week vacations at Mussoorie, in the high foothills of the Himalayas, one thousand miles north. Here was Woodstock School, founded primarily for missionary children, with a program from kindergarten through high school that was equal to the best American or European schools. Missionary mothers with children in school took turns spending a three-month period in our primitive guest apartment house, Prospect Point, so that children going to Woodstock could be in their own parents' care for three months of the nine-month term. This house was on a high ridge with a superb view of the vast two hundred mile sweep of the Himalaya to the north, and the Sewalik range of ancient hills and the limitless sweep of the Ganges-Jumna plain of North India to the south.

Missionary men would come up to spend their shorter leave with their families. The children stayed in the pleasant boarding school for six months of the year. Long vacation was from mid-December to mid-March, when the Mussoorie hills were often blanketed with deep snow.

Vacation at Mussoorie was refreshing. The crystal clear air, the crisp winds from the high snow ranges, the inviting hiking trails, inspiring worship services in English in the ecumenical atmosphere of Kellogg Memorial Church, opportunity to swap ideas with other missionaries from a dozen different countries and faith backgrounds, and time to read great books and hear good music, and play hard tennis provided us with an ideal vacation atmosphere.

However, we novices spent three months each of the first two years of our service in intensive language study at our hill station. In our years, there were about fifteen of us from several missions learning Gujarati, and a group of nearly a hundred learning Hindi. After our two terms of language school at Mussoorie, our son was ready for kindergarten, so that was our usual vacation place. The long hikes in the mountains, the exotic bazaars, the incomparable scenery made this a rewarding place and time of renewal. I was asked several times to be preacher for the ecumenical services at Kellogg Church, and also sang solos and gave chapel talks at Woodstock School.

A memorable expedition was the hike to the top of Nag Tibba, which I did twice. This involved dropping down four thousand feet through the deodar forests to the gorge of the Aglar River, then climbing through side canyons, hill villages and evergreen forests to the ten-thousand foot summit. It was a gruelling trip of twenty five miles each way. A young Canadian and I did it in a day and a half in our first year up there. Another favorite hike was to Dhanaulti, fifteen miles out along Tehri Road. A party of six, with two coolies to carry food and bedding made this trip once. At every turn in the trail there were magnificent views of the snow ranges, or the vast expanse of the plains far below us. During the night as we slept in our sleeping bags on the grass near the government bungalow, a big Himalayan bear raided a potato field on a terrace just below us. When the villagers who were guarding the field chased the bear, he charged right through our camp, driving us indoors for the rest of the night.

After a year in study and work at Anklesvar, we were to transfer to Vyara, fifty miles up the Tapti Valley from the sea, among the Gamete and Chaudra peoples, where some of our most successful mission work was in progress. We were delayed several months when I had to spend a month in Dahanu Hospital with a severe case of typhoid fever. Our only missionary doctor at the time was Dr. Barbara Nickey. Since the hospital was for women only, I was given an isolated corner room with a bit of veranda. Ilda stayed with the doctor and nurses in the adjoining mission house. During the quiet weeks of my slow recovery there, I went through a real spiritual crisis. We had come to India with such incandescent hope of years of useful ministry; I was acquiring a good command of the language, and Vyara seemed to need us. But here I was with a stubborn and almost fatal illness.

One night when I had tasted deep despair, my bed was wheeled out on the veranda where I could hear the rustle of the night breeze in the palms and mango trees and witness the moon rise like a great silver disk over the low hills nearby. In the quietness I suddenly had an overwhelming sense of the Presence of God by my side, and the words of Isaiah 41:10 seemed to be spoken to me in a resonant yet gentle voice, "Fear thou not; for I am with thee; be not dismayed; for I am thy God; I will strengthen thee; Yes, I will help thee; Yes, I will uphold thee with the right hand of my righteousness." A deep peace came to me, and I went quietly to sleep. I can honestly say that never since that holy night have I known a single hour of despair or of real discouragement!

We moved to Vyara in January 1933, and soon were absorbed in full-time activity. I was to be a counsellor to some twenty-five rural schools and four (later six) congregations scattered over an area of four hundred square miles of rich farmland and forests. Here there were over two thousand baptized Christians among a population of perhaps thirty-five thousand people. We were to spend the cool months each year, November through February, camping in the villages, assisting the teachers and pastors in every way we could, preaching and teaching. In addition, because the Indian Christians and their leaders were for the most part new in faith and experience and the mission was still inclined to be paternalistic, I had to care for the finances of our work, paying the teachers, seeing that the school buildings were repaired, securing text books and supplies. This meant a day each month meeting all the workers, counselling with them, paying their salaries, being advisor to their thriving cooperative society, arranging vacations, et cetera.

Our home base was a substantial stone house two miles from the little county seat town of Vyara, and from the railway station. We shared the house with a beautiful and highly motivated missionary, Olive Widdowson, who had already spent twenty-two fruitful years in India. She was in charge of the excellent boarding school for village girls which was adjacent to our home. A half mile away was a similar school for boys.

Our other colleagues at Vyara were Dr. and Mrs. J. M. Blough, who lived in the older house adjacent to the boys' school and the church. J. M. was a saintly, witty, quiet, scholarly theologian and Bible scholar, who had perfect command of the Gujarati language. Most of his time was spent in Bible translation, writing, editing the Sunday School lessons, and compiling a Gujarati hymnal. He was a most helpful senior colleague, always courteous, encouraging, and supportive. Gentle almost to a fault, he and his totally unselfish wife, Anna, had given themselves so completely to the Indian Christian community that they were looked up to as the "Mabop" (father and mother) of the total Christian community at Vyara. He and I complemented each other's work, for I was aggressive, inclined to be impatient, eager to experiment, uncomfortable with the paternalism which seemed so characteristic of the older missionaries.

We lived nearly five years at Vyara. The rural people here were good farmers, jolly, independent, and quite receptive to the Gospel. Most of the older Indian ministers and teachers had come from the orphanage phase of the mission activity about the turn of the century. A devastating famine had left scores of thousands of homeless, starving children in Western India. The mission built orphanages, and saved hundreds of these children, educating and parenting them. From this group were raised up a fine corps of able, dedicated Christian leaders. But at Vyara, there were young indigenous leaders arising, who were inclined to resent the greater influence these older leaders had.

Memories come flooding back to me of the busy Vyara years. The months camping in the villages were very happy. We needed an Indian co-worker, and God sent us a great one! Bolidas Naranji was a handsome young farmer-teacher about twenty-five years of age, with a beautiful shy wife named Manibai. He was an excellent singer and a devout Christian. He had taught a village school for a year or two, but one night while he and Manibai were at a Love Feast at Vyara, the more fanatical Hindus of the village burned his house. Discouraged, he went back to farming, but when he heard of our need for a fellow-worker he came to us. We worked and travelled and camped together two winters, shared most of our meals, and shared the preaching and teaching. When Bolidas played the "tabla," the resonant drums, and sang, the villagers came in great numbers, and he could stir them with the beautiful lyrics set to Indian ballad tunes. In each village he would organize a choir to do the folk dancing and singing which proved to be so effective in our work. He and I would talk with the farmers at their work, visit the schools, and then hold a meeting every evening.

After two years, this couple wished to return to a settled life teaching. He was invited to start a Christian elementary school at Pipalkuva, a big village where there had never been any school or any Christian work done. The village people built a house with two big rooms, one to live in, one for the school, and the young family moved there and started a school. Soon Bolidas had thirty children in school. His teaching was so winsome and effective that the children would come to school at daybreak, long before he rang the bell! And they came six days a week and on holidays. Soon with older brothers and sisters they thronged his Sunday School as well!

At the end of the year, we baptized nearly forty older youth and adults, who became a part of the thriving young Kikakui Church, six miles away across the hills. At Christmas time of Bolidas' second year in Pipalkuva, the young Christian group asked to have a Love Feast in the village. Of the six hundred villagers, about half were Gametes and half Chaudras, who were rival castes and would never eat together or mix socially. Bolidas and his young men prepared the meal and invited everyone to Love Feast! Near evening on the appointed day, some forty Christians from Kikakui arrived, walking through the teak forest. The ground in front of the school had been swept and the air was full of the aroma of spicy goat stew and a huge cauldron of rice steaming over a fire. At sunset the village people came. They sat on the ground in orderly rows, forgetting all about caste. More than three hundred men, women, and children were served the delicious stew and rice on plates made of sal leaves pinned together with thorns, and all ate together as a full moon rose over the Vindhya mountains beyond the Tapti River. Then the baptized Christians washed one another's feet, while all the non-Christians sat in amazed and reverent silence. The young pastor from Kikakui, Somchand Ukadbhai, and I served the communion—flat Indian barley bread, and juice from cooking raisins, which we spooned into outstretched right hands. When the service ended, Bolidas brought out his drums, cymbals and harmonium, and until long after midnight the night air was vibrant with singing and clapping as half-a-hundred youth sang and danced their new-found Christian joy! I have shared in hundreds of Love Feasts across the years, but none ever surpassed this in beauty, reverence and joyful celebration!

That winter, while we camped in Pipalkuva, we learned that a village across the Tapti River four miles away wanted us to visit in the hope that we could start a school there. Our Vyara pastor, Jivanji Haribhai, Ilda and I waded across the river, here about a hundred yards wide and only two feet deep, and walked a mile to the village. We were the first foreigners, and the first Christians ever seen in that village. Children hid and women stayed in their huts. But soon a crowd gathered; Jivanji and I talked with them, and we promised to find a teacher if they would erect a simple school and dwelling for him.

While at Vyara most of my work was with the village schools and churches. On the occasion of a field visit by Brethren Bonsack, Brubaker and Miller, we took them to the big village of Kikakui, ten miles from Vyara. The occasion was the organizing of a new congregation, baptism of some thirty persons, and a village Love Feast. A bit of excitement was added to the Love Feast when a big leopard was seen passing near by!

On the occasion of this visit by the American Mission Board members, I was appointed to accompany them on a visit to North India, to the area around Sialkot and Lahore where there had been phenomenal mass movements of rural folk largely from the outcaste Chumars into the Christian Church. This opportunity to study the work of Presbyterian missions there was particularly welcome to me because of my growing interest in rural evangelism. The whole missionary community had been stirred by the studies made by Bishop J. Waskom Pickett of the Methodist Church and his provocative report entitled "Christian Mass Movements in India."

The deep unrest and disillusionment among the outcastes and untouchables all over India made it seem likely that they might turn to Christianity in large numbers. In some areas they had done so, overwhelming the resources of the churches to prepare and teach them adequately. Bishop Pickett's study stressed the vast opportunity afforded the church by these movements, but also the crucial importance of adequate instruction, and providing life-transforming experiences of worship for the great companies of new believers.

We had high expectations that the conditions in the rural areas in which our mission worked could experience phenomenal growth also. At the same time, the holistic approach to life which we represented made it imperative that we concentrate on the improvement of the total life of the village people. We believed that Christ was concerned with the totality of life, and not just in saving men's souls! So, while I specialized in evangelism, the fruitful emphasis of the Vocational Training School and the entire mission in rural reconstruction, on relieving hunger and poverty, on better land use and preventive medicine, caused our work to move more slowly, but on a solid foundation.

Our kind of mission was, I think, deeply respected and appreciated by Indian leaders. During this period, Mahatma Gandhi was not only stirring the very foundations of India by his push for independence, he was also promoting cottage industries, better rural education, and the abolition of untouchables. He called the eighty million outcastes *Harijans*, the people of God. But his emphasis was to remove their disabilities, make them equal to low caste Hindus, and keep them Hindu! He was bitterly opposed to conversion and had little understanding of the dynamics of the Christian faith experience in transforming the total life of the people.

For a few years Dr. B. R. Ambedkar, a brilliant leader of the vast untouchable community, seemed to lean toward leading his people into Christianity. But the uneven quality of Christian community life and the powerful inducements of other religions finally led him to become a Buddhist and to advocate this religion.

My deep interest in rural evangelism and my proficiency in the language opened the door for some quite significant ecumenical service. I was made chairman of the evangelism committee of the Gujarat branch of the Bombay Representative Christian Council. With the blessing of our own mission, I was asked to tour all the areas of Gujarat in the interests of rural evangelism. For four months in 1936, I travelled among the Methodist, Presbyterian and Christian Missionary Alliance churches in this populus area, preaching and leading institutes and youth camps. I spoke about one hundred times in this period and found Indian Christians and missionaries alike deeply concerned to find new and better ways to witness to their neighbors.

One of the most glowing memories of this period is that of preaching the Easter sermon in the great Presbyterian Church in Ahmedabad. The singing was triumphant and marvelous, and to see the church completely filled and hundreds standing at the doors and windows to hear the Easter message inspired me to preach as I had rarely preached before!

Two years after beginning work in Vyara, a small group of Indian leaders and missionaries became concerned about the kind of training needed for ministry in the rural areas where the Church of the Brethren served. I remembered the complaint about Bible School graduates I heard in North India, that they came to the villages with long coats, soft hands, and huge Bibles, but unable to relate to village people. We feared that our own young men might be equally unready. As we studied Bishop Pickett's book and compared our ministerial training with the quality of education at the Vocational Training School, we felt a great need to completely revise the program of training for pastoral ministry.

In India and many other countries with growing young churches, there have been three levels of theological education. Bible Schools are the most elementary, always teaching in the vernacular; they offer two or three years of training to men and women who have primary school education; the emphasis has traditionally been heavy on Bible knowledge, with some training in preaching, teaching and evangelism. Theological Schools offer more advance training, requiring a high school education as prerequisite. Instruction is usually bilingual, in English and vernacular. These schools are usually inter-denominational and regional. The theological college, a true graduate institution, grants the theological degrees; in our time, Serampore was the only such college impowered to grant degrees. Two or three others were accredited but had their graduates receive the Serampore degrees.

Our Church of the Brethren Bible School had given quite thorough training across the years to all those who were serving as pastors and evangelists. At the urging of our group, the church and mission appointed a committee, Anna M. Warstler, P. G. Bhagat and I, to draw up a new design for the basic ministerial training.

We changed the name of the school to "Rural Church School," shortened the curriculum to two years, and changed the location to Vyara. For two years we had the first class of twelve students in residence there, and G. K. Satvedi, the veteran theologian of the Indian leaders, and I were the instructors. Some empty buildings of the boys' school were renovated for living quarters, and the classes were held in the beautiful and commodious Vyara Church. Most of our carefully selected students were married, and several of the wives also were full-time students.

Our schedule provided for seven months of intensive class work at Vyara. Satvedi taught the scripture courses and classes in devotional life and preaching. We had courses also in rural reconstruction, rural sociology, leading worship, teaching methods, et cetera. We brought in other Indian teachers or missionaries to offer intensive short courses in areas of their competence. Students were enthusiastic in their response. For the four months, January through April, the men students and I toured in the villages. This was intensely practical field experience. In the early mornings we had an hour or two of class instruction, and sharing about their work and witness in the villages. By April, as the heat became intense, we found the pace quite tiring and welcomed the month of May as vacation time. After the seven months of class work in the second year, the men and their families were placed in village church situations to try out their skills—we would call this an intern relationship now. In this field-work period, Brother Satvedi returned to his home in Bulsar and his many responsibilities in the larger church and his writing, while I spent my time visiting and supervising the students in their villages. Some students would have much preferred the more settled student life of the former Bible School, but most were enthusiastic about their new experiences. All of the men were employed upon graduation as village teachers or evangelists, where they carried responsibility for church growth and shepherding.

An outstanding experience of the first years' touring illustrates both the problems and rewards of this kind of witness. A great annual religious fair or *jattra* was held at the base of Devli Mardi, a nine hundred-foot wooded hill some fifteen miles from Vyara. About five thousand people gathered for the three-day celebration. Merchants spread out their wares, beggars and holy men came from far and wide. The young men and I pitched our tents under a big *pipul* tree at the base of the hill. On two evenings, we invited people to a meeting in which the men sang, witnessed, and we used slides, first on agriculture or health, then a presentation on the life and ministry of Jesus. About eight hundred people came and were deeply interested. The first full day, the young men circulated among the crowd, talking with people about the Christian way of life, giving many scripture portions, and selling many New Testaments. The Brahmin priests of the beautiful marble temple nearby invited me to come into their meeting room in the temple for conversation. Here, as we sat cross-legged on cushions, we talked, sharing faith and religious experiences. I was astonished at their hearty welcome, and that we could talk together for three hours!

On the last morning, all the men and boys — including the students and me — climbed the hill for the *puja*, the vision of the goddess. The "Bhagats," the leaders of the cult which held the festival, crawled into the little cave among the rocks where the goddesss was supposed to live, while the crowd chanted and sang outside. Soon the priests all came backing out hurriedly and ordered silence. The goddess would now speak! The big goat they had brought to sacrifice to her, already terrified, now in the sudden quiet let out a great "Baaaah!" Soon they cut his throat, poured blood around the sacred shrine, then roasted the goat and ate him!

Another incident on this tour made a deep impression on all of us. We camped in the beautiful forest village of Petaudra on the edge of the Dangs forest, twenty miles from Vyara. Here there was a strong Christian group with one of our ablest young ministers, Rupsingh Mangaldas, and his talented wife, Dhirajbai. The students fanned out through the village inviting everyone to our evening meeting.

Soon a group of them came hurrying back, saying that a girl on the far side of the village was demon-possessed and that a group of witch doctors had been torturing her for three days. Would I please come at once? They had tried to talk to her, but she had attacked them wildly, and the witch doctors were very hostile. The girl was robust, about eighteen years old. Her father finally tried to kill her, or to gouge her eyes out. In her frenzy she gashed her own throat and stomach with a sickle, and was a fearsome and pitiful sight. By the time I arrived at the threshing floor where all the excitement was centered, the witch doctors had decided to cart off the girl to a hilltop shrine to beat her to death, since they had not been able to exorcise the devils.

Fearing a terrible tragedy, I urged the village head man to call them back, which he quickly did. Soon the cart returned. When the girl Shanti (whose name ironically means *peace*) saw me, she jumped from the cart and ran toward me. The students were frightened, but as she threw herself on the ground at my feet she cried out, "Oh sir, help me! They are trying to kill me!" I assured her that no one would harm her now. As she calmed down her father came behind me with a big knife. The students restrained him, and as I placed my hands on Shanti's head, I prayed for her, that she might be made whole and find real peace. Soon she sat up, gathered her tattered, dirty sari around her, and seemed to come back to sanity again. We sent for Dhirajbai, the minister's wife, to come. Together we cleaned up the girl's ghastly, festering wounds and Dhirajbai helped her to bathe and dress. She stayed at the minister's home that night. The next morning they took her to the government doctor some ten miles away, who sent her back home, saying that she was a healthy girl and would heal up all right. The witch doctors went away muttering angrily.

This episode seemed to me quite like Jesus' healing the Gaderene demoniac. Surely it was His power that had driven out the demons of fear and frenzy from the poor village girl!

Because both Ilda and I had quite serious health problems, we were transferred to Bulsar in 1937, where we lived next door to Drs. Raymond and Laura Cottrell, and where we had their excellent care for the last two years of our stay in India. We moved our Rural Church School operation to Bulsar also, where the Bible School had good facilities from former years. Here we had an excellent class of fifteen men and fourteen wives, who carried through with great enthusiasm a two-year course similar to our first class at Vyara. Opportunities for field work were more limited here, but Brother Satvedi and Baxter Mow both helped greatly. Satvedi resumed the principalship of the school here and would carry it on when we left on our first furlough in March 1939.

In this class, one of the most responsive students was Bolidas, who had been with us at Vyara. When the class graduated, he made a moving speech of appreciation and announced that he and his family wanted to go to the most difficult place which could be found for his ministry. The church took him at his word. He was assigned to be minister-at-large and evangelist to the scattered lumber camps in the dense forsets of the Dangs district in the Western Ghatz, with his home base near our mission at Ahwa. Here he walked hundreds of miles through dense jungles where tigers and leopards were still abundant and often swam rivers infested with crocodiles, carrying his radiant witness by song and story to the isolated groups of Christians and the workers in the camps. He burned out his life in a few short years and died of tuberculosis by the time he was forty!

Two or three other developments occupied much of my time and thought in the later years of our service in India. Frank M. Laubach, the versatile Reformed Church missionary in the Phillipines, had developed a remarkably effective method of teaching adults to read their native languages. The success of his method there created demand for his help in many other areas of the world, including India. Our rate of literacy was less than ten percent, and about 1936, Laubach came to Gujarat and helped the Christian forces there to get started on his method. It proved to be an immediate success, and soon hundreds of adult literacy classes were progressing all over Gujarat. One of our young missionaries, Kathryn Kiracofe, specialized in literacy work throughout her career. One of the needs for the thousands of new readers was seen to be a simple periodical, and I was asked to create and edit such a paper. With the help of a number of Indian colleagues, we launched a four-page monthly rural newspaper and named it *Ajavaliu*. This word could mean a skylight in a village house, or the moonlit part of the month. But one of my Indian friends sardonically called it "Moonshine." The little paper carried news, articles on poultry raising, farm practices, health and child care, information about cooperative societies, and always some brief pieces about the Christian religion. All of us who worked on the paper did it as volunteer service. The price of the paper to subscribers was about one cent per copy, and we ran no deficits! It was distributed by the churches, so we had no postage expenses. I served as editor for the final two years of my time in India, and then an Indian editor took it over. It was still going well when I visited India in 1961!

Before we went to India, the church camping movement was well started in America and we had been involved in it at several camps. It seemed to us that Indian youth, too, might find camping a rich experience. While at Vyara, we worked with several pastors and teachers in planning a youth summer camp. The site was a grassy meadow beside a mile-long reservoir on a small river at Chikhli, six miles east of Vyara. Tents were pitched under great, spreading *muhada* trees. Here about fifty young people, boys and girls, with about eight teachers and our Vyara pastor, Jivanji Haribhai, spent a delightful week. In May, the temperature climbed to 115° nearly every day, so our classes and games were from six to ten in the morning, after morning prayers on the river bank at dawn and a quick morning tea.

On the first morning near noon, the boys and male teachers wanted to swim, and urged me to join them. We knew that at least two big crocodiles lived in the river, and I declined at first. The boys said they knew these "muggers," and that they only ate goats and fish, never humans! So I did join them, timidly. Though some of the stronger swimmers came close to a crocodile, no one was attacked! Often in the morning prayers, we could see the crocodile's huge eyes bulging curiously above the water a few yards from us! We concluded the week in camp with a very moving Love Feast service, led by our pastor. The tradition of church camps for youth has continued in the Indian Church. I was invited to share leadership also in a large camp for Methodist youth at Jubbulpore in Central India.

One of the cultural-recreational activities which gave me much satisfaction was participation in a male quartet: Lynn Blickenstaff, bass, A.F. Bollinger and Floyd Banker, a Wesleyan neighbor, tenors, and I as baritone. We sang often at mission conferences and in Bombay churches, did some radio broadcasting, and once provided music for a large spiritual life conference in Central India.

Perhaps the most far-reaching direction in my missionary career was a thorough study of worship. One memorable day in early 1935, I was boarding a train at Songhad, east of Vyara, when I met a distinguished Bengali Brahmin, Governor Mukerji of our province of Baroda state. He invited me to join him in his compartment for some good talk. This man was a distinguished scholar, a reverent student of the Christian scriptures, and a nephew of the Nobel Prize poet, Rabindranath Tagore. In the course of our long conversation, he said at one point, "Mr. Ziegler, I fear you are secularizing the life of the Indian peasant. In his ancestral religion, there are acts of worship and prayer and religious celebration of all the events and joys and tragedies of his everyday life. Religion and life are inseparable. When this farmer becomes a Christian, you tell him that worship is done on Sundays, in a special building. You ask him to sing hymns — translations of poems from a different culture, with tunes that grate on his ears. You ask him to give up his idols, but what do you give him as symbols of his new faith which he can understand? Why don't you use Indian forms and music, have Christian celebrations which relate to his daily life? If you do, his life will be much richer, and I believe he would be a better Christian!"

I felt that Mr. Mukerji's kindly but profound criticism was just, and creatively disturbing. I had long had deep concerns about making worship much more indigenous to Indian culture and more creative. My reading of Pickett's "Christian Mass Movements in India" strongly reinforced these growing concerns, for he had found that when the rapidly growing new churches where mass movements had occurred provided rich indigenous occasions for worship, the whole life of the new Christian communities was ennobled and changed. On the other hand, when worship was neglected or casual, little transformation of life took place.

As we began our new venture in ministerial training in the Rural Church School at Vyara, I shared my concerns with Indian leaders and missionaries, then with my students. In the school, we began to create with the students new worship forms and liturgies and had long discussions about the Christian celebration of their national and folk festivals. We believed that the forms of folk dance and music could be used with Christian lyrics. Our students were soon working out orders for all kinds of celebrations and forms of worship which would be truly indigenous. They were already using many Indian tunes, instruments, and folk dance patterns in their villages. Now in our months in the villages, we used many of the new forms and patterns and found village people enthusiastic in their response.

Though we knew that probably many others were experimenting in these directions, I was urged to prepare a book which would explain my concepts of worship and would also contain examples of the kinds of orders and forms which we had tried out. Bishop Pickett and some prominent Indian leaders gave me strong encouragement. I wrote the book in

1938, and entitled it simply, "A Book of Worship for Village Churches."
The Lucknow Publishing House, a Methodist press, printed a modest edition of the book, and soon it was selling well. Our Indian colleagues
thought it should be in the Gujarati language, too, so I immediately re-wrote it in that language. It was published by the Brethren mission and sold
for about twenty cents! Before we left India in March 1939, it was being
translated into several other Indian languages.

By a happy coincidence, Dr. John H. Reisner, the executive of
Agricultural Missions, Inc., was visiting the Lucknow press just as my book
was completed. He asked for a copy and read it en route to New York. Soon
I had a letter from him, praising the book highly, and asking my permission
to publish it for world-wide circulation by Agricultural Missions.

I was astonished by such a reception of the book and, of course,
gladly consented to its wider publication. In his newsletter to rural mis-sionararies around the world, Dr. Reisner recommended the use of the
book and its translation as an example of what should be done in all the
younger churches. Though I do not have accurate figures, there were two
or three re-printings of the book in English, and it was translated into
more then twenty languages in Asia, Africa, and Latin America. Many
years later, I frequently met Christian leaders from many countries who
had read it! The acceptance of this book opened doors to much future op-portunity for leadership and writing in this area of church life.

Earlier I related my experience with severe illness. All my life until
then, I had enjoyed robust health. But through the rest of our term in In-dia, I suffered frequent severe bouts of malaria and one major surgery.
The malaria attacks were often debilitating, and several times I spent a
few days in the hospital at Bulsar. Fortunately I always bounced back
quickly! One good by-product of the attacks, along with a rigorous pro-gram of long walking and cycle tours in my work at Vyara, was that my
average weight through those years was one hundred forty-five pounds.

Ilda also suffered much from malaria, but more ominously, in late
1933 and early 1934 her health seemed to deteriorate rapidly. She spent
some weeks with the good doctors in Bulsar. Finally, as the mission con-ference began in early March, she became very ill and lapsed into a deep
coma, which was discovered to be diabetic. Massive use of insulin brought
her back slowly to consciousness. There were many fervent prayers for her.
As she slowly regained strength, she, too, went through her Gethsemane
of despair. The doctors had us read everything in their library about
diabetes. They tried to encourage us, but at the same time told us that
with good care she might well live a good normal life for another ten years!
After a week of her slow recovery, I had to return to my duties at Vyara.
Drs. Cottrell thought Ilda should stay with them several more weeks, then
go to the invigorating climate of the Himalayas in a fine sanatorium for
several months. We accepted their plan, and our five-year-old Robert
went with another family and a group of missionary children to enter

kindergarten at Woodstock School.

In mid-May, I also went to the mountains, and Ilda was—somewhat reluctantly—released from the sanatorium. We never so deeply appreciated our life together as in the weeks that followed, as we walked among the deodar forests and found her strength coming back rapidly in the sharp, winy breezes from the high Himalaya.

I was always amazed at Ilda's ability to discipline herself to the rigid diet and regular use of insulin in the years that followed. Though she often had severe complications from diabetes, she led a vigorous and wholesome life. Instead of the ten years the doctors had tentatively promised us, Ilda stayed with me and lived a wonderfully complete and beautiful life for thirty-six years after the onset of her diabetic affliction.

Our son thrived and grew in his early schooling at Woodstock and was a source of great joy and pride when he was with us in the long vacations. Fortunately his health always was excellent! He was nine years old when we sailed for our homeland in early March 1939, old enough to get immense delight from the life on shipboard and in our two weeks' vacation in Italy, Switzerland, Paris and London.

There are many significant or vivid experiences which come to my mind as the seven years in India are recalled. A few of them, not in any important sequence, are these:

Sixteen months after arrival in India I was elected moderator of the annual conference of the first India District. This meant taking the chair immediately and conducting all the business in Gujarati. I had excellent help from Indian leaders and missionaries alike.

On one occasion I had a delightful conversation with Mahatma Gandhi, when he was leaving one of his ashrams at Bardoni, near Vyara. We also had some correspondence when I invited him to write for *Ajavaliu*. He refused!

Ilda, Bobby, a group of Indian colleagues and I had a memorable journey to attend the Marathi District Meeting at Ahwa, fifty-five miles from Vyara. We travelled three days mostly on foot, through spectacular tiger-infested jungles to reach Ahwa.

I recall many rugged journeys. One trip to visit the Vyara area schools and churches during the monsoon season took twelve days, 160 miles on foot, often crossing swollen rivers. I noted that I helped to eat twenty-two chickens on this trip—and spoke never a word in English!

One of our young teachers in that area became deranged and went on a rampage destroying old idols on Songadh Mountain. I went to court to plead that he be released as a harmless and sick person. However he was sent to prison for two years.

Our Vyara home had both perils and blessings. We often killed kraits, foot-long pencil-thin venomous snakes inside our house. But outside, we several times watched up to 800 or 900 big juicy mangoes ripening on a tree near the bungalow.

One memorable and historic event happened near us, When the Indian National Congress met near Vyara I attended a full day, hearing and meeting Jawaharlal Nehru, his sister, Mrs. Pandit, the present prime minister, Morarji Desai, and mingling with the orderly crowd of more than two hundred thousand from all over India.

Our journeys by train to the high hills for vacation were always interesting. One that proved especially lively included a leisurely conversation with a beautiful Moslem woman who threw back her veil and conversed with me in perfect English! This just wasn't done! Her husband soon joined in the good talk. He was finance minister of a central Indian state, and she was a close friend of Canadian missionaries whom I knew well.

I have written of the invigorating vacations at Mussoorie. I remember a fantastic walk from Mussoorie to the Jumna River with Ralph Townsend. We ate a big mahseer, a fine game fish which a local fisherman caught for us. Then we slept under the stars, while leopards came coughing down to the river to drink near us.

The work of our missionary doctors is most impressive. After thirty years of sevice the Drs. Cottrell still showed the compassion of the healing Christ. Dr. Raymond one day showed me a baby girl already hopelessly blind because her parents had tried to cure her sore eyes by applying ashes and cow dung, bringing her to the hospital too late. There were tears in his eyes as he explained the baby's plight.

When we lived in Bulsar, we were often treated to the powerful aroma of Bombay Duck (a small deep sea fish) drying on the beach three miles away. Often in the villages I shared fish stew using these fish, with our Indian friends.

After Kathryn Kiracofe and Rachel and Earl Ziegler completed their language examination, we helped celebrate with a picnic on a mountain near Bulsar. On our way home we experienced a wild runaway of our swift young oxen when the driver got drunk! Earl and I wrestled the oxen down, and we walked home.

A source of deep satisfaction to me was in helping our village congregations to build simple but beautiful little mud and bamboo meetinghouses and securing some mission funds to provide tile roofs for them.

Finally, a word of evaluation of our work in India. It was no accident that, in a conference with a noted foreign journalist, Prime Minister Jawaharlal Nehru excepted the Brethren, the Friends, and the Mennonites from his scathing criticism of Christian missions in general. When India should become independent, he said, he would ask all but those three to leave. For these small missions really were in India to serve, and were truly sympathetic servants of the Indian people!

I believe that the holistic approach to salvation, the close and brotherly relationships with our Indian sisters and brothers, our identification with the total life and aspirations of the Indian people, constituted a valid and genuinely Christian approach. None of our missionaries fitted the caricature of a stiff, cold foreigner under a palm tree with a big Bible. We made our mistakes. We were still Westerners in dress and habits. But I believe our love was genuine, deep and evident.

The church established by the Brethren has had its vicissitudes, its internal dissensions, its defections, and at times its quarrels with their brothers and sisters from America. But it became a strong church, a truly Indian church, which has taken a creative part in the emerging Church of North India. From its very beginnings, the Church of the Brethren mission in India was made up of men and women for others. They were well-rounded Brethren Service workers years before the term was conceived for our response to world suffering. Reconcilers always, they had the confidence and trust of the leaders of the great non-violent movements for Indian freedom.

My acquaintance with Brethren outreach also in China and Africa, and my firsthand knowledge of our work in India, lead me to say that this movement is one of the noblest and most permanently helpful ministries the Brethren have ever undertaken!

Even though Ilda and I both had serious health problems while we lived in India, which prevented our return for longer service, the seven and one-half years we spent there were a most rewarding experience. We both loved the gentle, courteous people of India. We came to have profound respect for the long ages of history behind them, the wealth of culture, the sturdy, independent resourcefulness of the peasants, their creative and non-violent struggle for national freedom. We loved the land—the austere and chaste beauty of the mighty Himalaya, the stately life-giving rivers, the luxuriant fields and gardens, the brooding ruins of civilizations long vanished into dust, the ethereal beauty of ancient buildings like the Taj Mahal, and the extravagant splendor of Hindu and Jain temples. India is a great land with a long and absorbing history, peopled by hundreds of millions of beautiful persons.

The Christian faith we tried to share is indeed the crown of Hinduism and Buddhism. From the richness of India's heritage we may confidently expect insights and lifestyles which may greatly enrich the thought and life of the whole Church of Christ.

CHAPTER 7

Does Life Begin at Forty?

*W*hen I was a boy, I somehow got the impression that when a person reached the age of forty, he had far passed his prime and was "over the hill." But about the time this decade of the 1940s began, I read a book entitled, "Life Begins at Forty," and I began to hope! As life's drama unfolded, these years, 1941 to 1951, proved to be full, busy and creative beyond my boldest dreams. I thought that since we could not return to India, God might have a hard time fitting us into some place secondary in His plan for us. I should have known better! He always plans far more wisely and largely than we expect.

In the chapter on my training for ministry, I told of our full year at Bethany Seminary upon our return from India. In addition to the heavy load of class work I carried that year, I did a great deal of deputation work, speaking for missions. In the first five months of our furlough we travelled extensively speaking in many churches, and during the year at seminary, many invitations came to talk in missions and to preach in churches and colleges. This was an intensely busy and productive year.

At the conclusion of the brief summer term at Bethany, in July 1940, we took off in our aging Plymouth for the summer of church camp leadership on the Pacific coast. This was our first trip west of the Rockies, and it was a combination of seeing majestic scenery and crowded teaching schedules for both of us in five summer camps, Beulah and Greenhorn in California, Myrtlewood in Oregon, Lost Lake in Washington, and Stover in Idaho. In these camps we got to know and like hundreds of Brethren people in an area quite new to us, and friendships were made which have lasted nearly forty years. These western camps were all family camps, a pattern which we found very congenial. After the five weeks of camp leadership, we spent two glorious weeks exploring the grandeurs of Yosemite and Yellowstone National Parks as we made our way back to Chicago.

While in our first week of camping, among the coastal redwoods at Camp Beulah near Santa Cruz, California, we had to decide our future place of ministry. I had visited First Church in York, Pennsylvania, early in July to explore the pastorate there. At Camp Beulah, we received a letter from Dr. Paul Bowman asking me to consider a call to become executive secretary for the Southeastern Region of the Church. Ilda and I spent several hours away from camp in a grove of redwoods, talking and praying. When we returned to camp, we believed we had clear guidance from the Holy Spirit, and we wrote two letters, one of gratitude and regret to Dr. Bowman, one of acceptance of the call to York.

For our Robert, now ten, the summer was a great adventure. He never met a stranger, and like Will Rogers, he never met a man he didn't like! In the parks we had close encounters with bears, deer and many other animals. One evening in Yellowstone, we joined a group which was herded carefully into an enclosure on a hillside hoping to see grizzly bears coming to a garbage dump. Forty-two came that evening! I began taking 35mm color pictures that summer. Nearly forty years later, this is still a major hobby!

Arriving back in Chicago at the end of August, we packed our things, bought a small homemade trailer, and started for Pennsylvania to begin our new pastoral duties. On the way, we talked much about the future. In some ways we were apprehensive about going to York. The congregation was large, about eight hundred members. And it was conservative, many members still adhering to strict Brethren garb. I would be required to wear what then passed as Brethren clerical garb. It even seemed necessary for Ilda to hide her plain wedding ring which she had worn since embarking for India nine years earlier. The work would be hard, for the church was still badly torn by dissension. Four years earlier, a tragic division had occurred. The pastor and some two hundred fifty members loyal to him had left and started a new congregation, meeting in a club house just six blocks from First Church. In the four years prior to our coming, Elder S. S. Blough had served as an interim pastor. M. R. Zigler, still ministry and home mission secretary, had recommended us to the church, and he told me afterward that he hoped I could stay as much as three years to get the congregation together again!

The York Church had no parsonage. The first three of our five years there we rented housing out of our rather meager salary. After two brief periods in unsatisfactory apartments in the city, one of the most gracious women of the church rented to us her comfortable home in the country, three miles from the church. Unfortunately, after a year in this lovely place, wartime restrictions on gasoline made it necessary to move back to York.

Soon after that, the church bought the comfortable duplex next door to First Church and we moved into our first parsonage for the final two years of our stay.

Though there were many families in this church who had comfortable incomes and substantial homes, the church was just emerging slowly from the "free ministry" phase and was not lavish in support of the pastor. We received $1680 per year at first. The salary was soon raised to $2000 per year and remained at that figure. There was no car allowance, and we paid our own rent until we moved into the new parsonage! However, many persons were generous in occasional gifts of food supplies and in their warm hospitality.

Another evidence of the congregation's ambivalence about having a professional pastor was revealed in an early conversation with a banker who was also an ordained minister and an influential member of the pastoral committee. "Brother Ziegler, you must realize that we here believe in the free ministry," he said. "There are seven of us ministers here. We all are in business or professions and don't have time for pastoral work. So we hired you to do pastoral work six days a week and expect you to take your turn with us preaching as a free minister on Sunday!" Obviously most of the congregation did not entirely share his views, for though I did usually spend six days a week caring for the pastoral duties and studying, I found that I was expected to preach twice each Sunday!

Years earlier, the congregation had established a mission in East York, and shortly before my arrival had dedicated a beautiful and functional church building, calling it Second Church. About one fifth of the eight hundred member congregation centered in this branch of the church. After two years of my pastorate, Second Church, with the blessing of the mother church, became a congregation in its own right with their own pastor and program. Relationships with Madison Avenue, the congregation which had broken away in 1936, gradually became more cordial, and the pastor and I developed a warm friendship.

Very soon after our arrival in York, we encountered serious problems with Ilda's health. While on our western trip, we had a frightening experience when she for the first time experienced severe insulin shock. Within a week after coming to York, she had several more and was hospitalized for a week to get her balance restored.

Soon after this experience, our new family doctor after careful examination gave us a shock. "Mrs. Ziegler, you are pregnant! That's the reason for the insulin shocks!" We were stunned. Ilda was past forty, and the probability of having this child, we were told, was extremely slim. We had been married sixteen years and had no hope left of becoming parents biologically! The ensuing months were anxious indeed. But on April 2, 1941, she gave birth to a beautiful, perfectly healthy, baby boy whom we named Donald Mark. Though Caesarian birth was necessary, Ilda and the little son were soon home and doing exceedingly well. This critical time and its anxieties seemed to deepen the warmth and love of the congregation for their new pastor and his family.

Now we had two lively boys, but we still longed to have a daughter. In January of 1945, a healthy baby girl was born to a teen-age unwed mother in the York Hospital. Through a Lutheran pastor friend who knew the family, arrangements were quickly made for us to take the baby. When she was nine days old we brought her home, and as soon as the necessary legal steps could be taken we adopted her, naming her Ruth Ann.

The York Church had immense potential and was ready and eager to move forward. Up until now, the church had never used musical instruments in worship, but the congregational singing was hearty and inspiring. There were excellent singing ensembles, and the appreciation for good hymns and ensemble singing was high. Some time after our arrival, a progressive young adult Sunday School class wanted to buy an organ for the church, and asked permission to do so. At a council meeting when the question came up, nearly three hundred people were present, and the debate was spirited and intelligent. The vote to accept the organ was about a three-fourths majority vote. One or two families who had most earnestly opposed the change left the church to go to more conservative congregations.

As time passed, the more progressive group of active members took courage and came into more and more positions of leadership. Though the church remained conservative, we could sense increasing tolerance for more liberal views and deeper unity. My ministry there spanned the World War II years, with all of the national tensions and problems of that era. But the congregation's support of an uncompromising stand against war never faltered. There were some tensions, for of the sixty to seventy young people who were caught up in the war, half went into Civilian Public Service as conscientious objectors, one went to prison for not co-operating with the draft, about a dozen accepted non-combatant service in the armed forces, and the rest were drafted or volunteered for regular military service.

When a small group of young men came to a Love Feast in their military uniforms, a minister and a few deacons approached me, suggesting that we ask them not to come to the Lord's Table. I told them that if these young men could not commune, I would not and would leave the sanctuary with them! When our young people came home on furlough, no matter what form of service they were in, there was no break in the deep comradeship they had always shared.

Our young people in Civilian Public Service were scattered widely, many in the forest camps, some in dairy herd testing, and a large group were serving in mental hospitals, most of them in Connecticut. The congregation heartily approved my pastoral visits to our youth whenever possible. In 1944-45, we had eight in Connecticut mental hospitals, several in Navy installations in New England, and one, Ernest Lefever, in Yale Divinity School. Ernest took the initiative in planning a Love Feast for all these young people in New England and I was asked to conduct the service. It was held in the Social Hall of an Episcopal Church at the edge of the Yale Campus. All of our York young people in the area came, several other Brethren students at Yale, and a group of Yale Divinity School professors and non-Brethren students shared in this moving worship experience. The Yale historian, Roland Bainton, participated in the service, and two or three black graduate students helped to make it truly ecumenical.

On this trip I visited two of the hospitals where our young people were stationed, visited several classes at Yale Divinity School, and lectured to a group of Divinity School students who were particularly interested in the rural church.

Our young people in the Civilian Public Service camp at Kane, in northern Pennsylvania, urged me to visit them also. This was in cold, high forest country, and temperatures often went to $-30°$F. I made my visit in early March and planned to spend a day in the woods with the boys. So I bought a suit of heavy woolen underwear to wear. But the day I arrived there was a thaw, temperatures were in the 50's, and I itched miserably! But the fellowship with the men in camp, and the good evening sessions with all the men made the trip a most pleasant one.

Only a few churches in the Southern Pennsylvania District had professional pastors in this period, and we were given large district responsibilities. I served both on the Board of Christian Education and the Ministerial Board. The Board of Education was greatly interested in a strong youth program, including camping. Eastern Pennsylvania District held youth conferences on the Elizabethtown College campus, but the time was ripe for a joint effort to establish a good church camp. Three men from our district were appointed to work with a similar group from Eastern District to establish a camp. Elder Ira Gibble, of the Little Swatara Church, helped us to find and purchase an old farm ideally situated at the base of the Blue Mountain near Bethel, some two hundred acres, half in fields and meadows, half in healthy timber land reaching up to the slopes of Blue Mountain on the north, and a smaller ridge to the south. We named it Camp Swatara, and when our districts approved the purchase, we began to lay plans for its development. There were several old farm buildings in good condition, ample wilderness areas for superb natural setting for camps, twenty-seven pure water springs and a creek which could be dammed for swimming.

Ilda and I helped in leadership for the first youth camps at Swatara. One of my assignments was to identify and mark varieties of trees and shrubs. I found over one hundred species that first summer! Since then Southern Pennsylvania has developed its own camp site and program, and Camp Swatara has had a far-reaching ministry for people of all ages.

The church in York was generous in its giving for outreach. During my years there, the Church of the Brethren gave large sums to support the Civilian Public Service program, the rapidly growing need for relief of the victims of war, and still maintained a vigorous program of overseas and home missions. For three of our five years there, First Church gave more money for the combined service and mission programs of the denomination than any other congregation, regardless of size!

During the last two years of my pastorate in York, I served also as instructor in Bible in York Collegiate Institute, a fine private junior college. An additional ministry was the opportunity to broadcast frequent radio devotional programs.

Seven young men of the congregation were licensed to the ministry in these years. Of this group, three, Arthur Hess, Donald Hursh, and Jesse Jenkins, have been pastors; Jack Melhorn, a college professor and president; John Eichelberger, the treasurer of Bethany Theological Seminary; Ernest Lefever, a distinguished scholar now teaching in Georgetown University; and Dr. Roy Pfaltzgraff has for more than thirty years been in Nigeria where he has become one of the world's leading authorities on the treatment of Hanson's Disease (leprosy).

When we terminated our work in York, it was with a satisfying sense of achievement! The church had grown in membership, but far more in global and spiritual awareness. It was more united, had developed many strong lay leaders, sent out some of its best young people into wider ministries, and was truly a great, stable, caring community of faith!

We left York in August 1945, with three fine youngsters, a small load of used furniture, little money, an aging car, and a host of friends!

When I was approached by President V. W. Schwalm of Manchester College to join the faculty, teaching courses in Bible and Christian Education, a combination of weariness and achievement at York, made the offer seem attractive. My teaching at York Collegiate Institute had been a joy and a stimulus to my intellectual growth. I resigned the pastorate, and at the end of August 1945 a Brethren Service truck moved us to North Manchester, Indiana. We bought a small house across the Eel River from the town, a mile from the college. Our Bob had had two years of high school in York and easily transferred to the rural Chester High School near our home. I could easily walk or ride my bicycle to the college.

I found the college atmosphere exhilarating. My senior colleague, Dr. Robert H. Miller, taught the more advanced Bible courses and philosophy. Since a Bible survey course was required of all students, I had large classes in two sections. Many of my students had come from quite conservative churches, and my moderately liberal stance in Bible interpretation and theology led to some real confrontations. I outlined and taught courses in Christian Education, Religious Art Appreciation,

Youth Work in the Church, Comparative Religion and a course in basic preparation for ministry. I quickly found that some of a college teacher's most important work is individual counselling with his students, and soon many hours were occupied in this activity. In those years regular chapel attendance was compulsory, and leading a chapel service was a challenging task. As I recall the programs I led, two of the most appreciated were a dramatic reading of the Book of Jonah and a reading of James Weldon Johnson's "St. Peter Relates an Incident," when Professor Paul Halladay joined me by singing "Deep River," as he came up the aisle to the stage at the dramatic climax of the poem.

President Schwalm was a competent administrator and a dedicated churchman, though he frequently seemed to become discouraged and anxious. Often he invited me to his office to talk over problems and join him in prayer. When at the end of two years of teaching I decided to return to the pastoral ministry, he expressed deep disappointment and even some anger at my decision. But I have always felt a real debt of gratitude to him for giving me this opportunity for a rich college teaching experience.

One of the dreams of President Schwalm shared with Dr. Miller and me was that of offering to pastors and churches in the college territory extension courses that would be helpful in their ministry. His thought was that my teaching load in the college should be light enough that I could carry much of this extension program. I taught a class on Old Testament prophets over a period of several months for a group of Indiana churches. Also Professor Halladay and I conducted several weekend institutes on music and worship in Ohio and Indiana.

We found the Manchester Church a warm and supportive fellowship. I served a year as Sunday School superintendent. Here, too, and on the faculty of the college, we formed lasting friendships. In addition to President Schwalm, the professors who taught me most and with whom I had closest comradeship were R. H. Miller, Charles Morris of the Physics Department, Edward Kintner, who was a strong churchman and biology professor, Paul Halladay, head of the music faculty, and the dean of students, Russell Bollinger. J. I. Baugher and John Boitnott were both teaching there while I was, and both went to Bridgewater College — Baugher as president in 1946 and Boitnott as dean in 1947, the same year I moved.

In the spring of 1947, I was asked whether I would be interested in a call to the college church in Bridgewater, Virginia. Although the two years as a college teacher were happy years, Ilda and I decided that the place where I could best exercise my ministry was in the local church rather than the college. I resigned from the faculty and accepted the call to the Bridgewater Church. The two years of teaching, I believe, were also a good learning experience and greatly enriched my ministry. At the end of the teaching years, I also received my theological degree from Bethany

Seminary. Bob graduated from high school, and Donald from kindergarten!

The good experience we had in the Bridgewater Church in our college years twenty years earlier, made the call to Bridgewater especially appealing. We already had many friends there, and I think my short period of college teaching had given me a good preparation for ministering to a college community.

The Bridgewater Church was and still is a unique combination of intellectual community, farm families, and a large number of retired persons. Diverse in interests, the congregation is close-knit geographically. Ninety-five percent of my pastoral calls were within a radius of two miles from the church! And in our little church directory booklet, there were three pages of Millers!

We arrived in Bridgewater with our family and possessions in June, and travelled on at once to the 1947 Annual Conference in Orlando, Florida. Ilda's mother, Etta Fike Bittinger, now made her home with us and went with us to Conference. Father Bittinger had died in 1938. Mother was very active, obsessed by work, and her children often remarked that they had to work harder than ever when she was there to "help" them!

I was installed as pastor at Bridgewater in early July, 1947, and promptly had a severe attack of mumps, which kept me from preaching my first sermon as pastor until July 27. Having a few weeks before the college year began gave me time to get acquainted with the rural and town members of the congregation. All through my pastoral ministry, I have tried to bring as much help and comfort as I could to the aging and suffering. There were several such persons at Bridgewater, and my time spent with them brought as much inspiration to me as I could ever give to them. President Baugher had a severe heart attack a few months before my arrival, and I visited him often. Later in the year he suffered an even more severe attack and had to resign the presidency of the college.

One invalid who helped me to grow was Tom Hollen. When we were students there, Tom was an active layman, ran a mill, and taught one of the most interesting Bible classes I had ever shared in. Now he was paralyzed and helpless. My visits with him were a delight — always a lot of good, wise counsel from him, some witty stories, and a deeply appreciated time of prayer. One cold winter day I had been out calling several hours before coming to his home. The temperature in his room was in the 80's, and I became drowsy. When I was about to leave, he asked me to offer a prayer. I started — and dozed off, my words trailing off incoherently. I caught myself awake and finished my prayer. Tom's twinkle of amusement showed that he knew what had happened, but it didn't spoil our friendship!

When college began, I made every effort to become acquainted with students and to attend college functions. Student attendance and interest in our services of worship was most gratifying. Though many resident students went home frequently on weekends, leaving two to three hundred on campus, we usually had one to two hundred or more in the services. With the approval of the church board, we worked out a plan to invite students to enroll as student members of the congregation, which we did annually. Nearly a hundred students accepted such membership. It was a special pleasure to have close ties with pre-ministerial students and attend their meetings. A few times, we offered special courses for college students. One which was especially well-received was on dating and preparation for marriage.

It must be said that it was difficult to keep a proper balance between my work with students and with the permanent congregation, and occasionally I was told that I spent too much time at the college. Among my most trusted counsellors in the church-pastor relationship were such men as retired Professor N. D. Cool, who was moderator of the church; D. C. Craun, a wise, gracious, influential deacon and farmer; Dr. Marshall Wolfe, professor of religion and next-door neighbor; C. B. and Lera Smith, who also lived next-door, he a retired minister in his upper eighties and she a wise and gracious counsellor.

Dr. Warren D. Bowman came as president of the college in 1949. With his experience as a pastor and churchman, he and his wife Olive became close friends and steadfast supporters of the church's ministry.

Much of the beauty and exaltation of our worship at the church was due to the wonderful team I had to work with—Professor Nelson T. Huffman, long-time choirmaster, and head of the college music department, and Ruth S. Weybright, a brilliant, sensitive organist and college teacher. Both had uncanny ability in selecting the right music for the services and were most gracious to work with.

Among our closest friends and co-workers were Nevin and Virginia Fisher, who lived two doors from us. Nevin was a gifted pianist, a college professor, and a philosopher. Virginia was the Director of Christian Education for the Southeastern Region, and a competent theologian. She and Ilda, with two other dedicated educators, Nancy Flory and Etta Bowman, were a team which did a great deal of promotion of better nurture for children of the churches. Among other methods which they used to promote the cause, they used role-playing and dramatic skits. Ilda often played the role of the over-worked Sunday School teacher or perplexed mother who just couldn't understand jargon or complex plans, and would appeal to the experts to simplify and clarify! They put on workshops in many places and not only awakened great interest but had great fun doing it!

One cold, clear winter night Nevin had given a piano concert at the college. When they came home Virginia had to address a stack of letters to go out to the churches in the morning. Nevin offered to take the letters to the post office a half-mile away, after midnight. Still in his tuxedo and an overcoat he went off briskly. As he told it, down on the street he saw a little black cat shivering on the sidewalk. He stooped to pet it and found it wasn't a kitty at all! When he arrived home, Virginia made him undress and leave all his skunk-perfumed clothes on the back porch. Unfortunately, he kept his shoes on, and put them under their bed! Ilda later put the episode into verse and read it to the faculty wives' club, to Virginia's embarrassed delight!

June 17, 1949, was a memorable day in Bridgewater and the surrounding area. That afternoon tremendous cloudbursts inundated the Shenandoah mountains to the west, and in fact for sixty miles of the mountain area. Vast landslides rushed down the mountain slopes, and soon a huge wall of water, mud and debris broke from the gap in the first ranges, and swept down North River. About midnight the river broke into its ancient bed near Round Hill, and a ten-foot wall of water swept over much of the little town. Two-thirds of the homes were flooded, some completely demolished. Two women and a little girl were washed away and drowned. We were at Annual Conference at Ocean Grove, New Jersey, at the time. Nelson Huffman, then mayor of Bridgewater, received the news the next day and at once started for home. When we arrived home Monday morning, the devastation was terrible to see. Our home was one of two on Broad Street which had little damage.

The next day I conducted the funeral of one of our church women, a near neighbor, who had perished in the flood, and a week later, the service for a nine-year-old girl whose body had just been found. That whole summer was a time of cleaning up and rebuilding. On Sunday the twenty-sixth of June, farmers planned to come from all over Rockingham County with their trucks and machinery to help clean up. Since three of the five churches in the town had serious flood damage, the ministers planned a union service in the college's Cole Hall for early that day, inviting our guest helpers to come also. Everyone came in boots and overalls, including the ministers! I preached on "When the Rains Came!" I spent the rest of the morning shoveling mud out of the basement of the Methodist Church. In the afternoon, I was asked to direct traffic at the main cross street in town, keeping sightseers moving and out of the way of trucks and tractors! Disasters can draw people close together and bring out great floods of compassion and helpfulness, as we discovered that day.

During Bob's junior year in college, four young men of the congregation were licensed to the ministry in a very impressive service. Myron Miller, who later succeeded his father as the executive of the Virginia Council of Churches; Byron and Dan Flory, twin sons of the veteran China missionaries, the Byron Florys, who both became successful pastors; and our son, Bob. The Florys, Bob, Earle Fike, David Rogers, Merle Crouse and several others in their class all went off to Bethany Theological Seminary after their 1951 graduation.

A few family events were important to us in the latter years of our pastorate in Bridgewater. Our son Robert and Connie Arbogast, a 1949 alumna of the college, were married in June, 1950. And a few months earlier, I performed the marriage ceremony for Ilda's mother and Elder William E. Sanger of Cordova, Maryland. Both were seventy-two years old, and they had twenty good years together after that!

For two of our four Bridgewater years our family life was enriched by having students live with us. One year it was a student minister girl, Edith Cosner, from Maryland. The next year it was a brilliant German exchange student, Renate Schulz.

During the decade of the forties, I became greatly involved in denominational and ecumenical work and in writing. When Annual Conference of 1941 voted to accept membership in the Federal Council of Churches, and the World Council then in process of formation, I was elected as one of the five representatives of the Church of the Brethren to the Federal Council and was chosen to represent us on its executive committee. Since I lived in York, Pennsylvania, at that time, it was easy to get to New York several times a year for meetings of the committee. The biennial meetings of the Federal Council which I attended were in Cleveland and Pittsburgh, during the years of World War II. At both of these meetings there were determined efforts by such men as Dr. Daniel A. Poling to get the council to give strong support to the war.

I am proud of the fact that the eloquent presentation of the Brethren peace position by Rufus D. Bowman, Paul Bowman and others helped the council to a more nearly Christian stance. After one such debate, the hundreds of delegates gave Rufus Bowman a standing ovation for his powerful presentation of the peace church position and our opposition to the war hysteria! My experience there, and years later as a delegate to the Third Assembly of the World Council of Churches, have firmly convinced me that the Brethren need to take forthright stands, and that when we do we are respected and heard. Though one of the smaller denominations in the Councils, we have exercised a salutary influence far out of proportion to our size. Far from being contaminated by our membership in the Councils, we have exerted strong influence; and in many areas of church life and faith, we have also learned much!

One year I served on the nominating committee of the Federal Council. When our committee met in New York, we all felt strongly the guidance of the Holy Spirit in a remarkable oneness of conviction. All five members of that committee came feeling that the courageous Bishop G. Bromley Oxnam of the Methodist Church should be nominated for president of the council and that a black man should be vice president. In a very short time we agreed on the nomination of Dr. Benjamin Mays, a noted negro educator from Atlanta. These two powerful leaders were elected, and their two-year administration was among the best the council ever had.

Throughout these years, I had a close and productive relationship with Dr. John H. Reisner of Agricultural Missions, Inc. Because of the wide distribution of the *Book of Worship for Village Churches,* and my work in India, I was invited to be worship leader for the Annual Meeting of the Foreign Missions Conference of North America at Swarthmore College, June 10-13, 1940. The liturgies and meditations I prepared for that conference were later published in a booklet by the Foreign Missions Conference. Dr. Reisner felt that the flood of interest created by the worship book should lead to additional publications. I collected creative liturgies and orders of worship from many lands and Agricultural Missions, Inc. published them in book form in 1943 as "Rural People at Worship." The Commission on Worship of the Federal Council asked me to write a booklet for American rural churches, along the lines of my work in the *Book of Worship.* This little book of forty-eight pages, entitled "Country Altars," was published in 1947.

The next year, growing out of my work preparing materials for family worship published by the Brethren Publishing House in the *Gospel Messenger* and the *Teachers' Monthly,* they asked me to prepare a booklet on family worship. This forty-eight page booklet, "Worship in the Christian Home," was published in 1943 by The Brethren Press, and enjoyed several reprintings over a number of years.

Dr. Reisner believed that the collection and periodic distribution of liturgies, prayers and orders of worship from rural churches around the world would be of creative service. For several years I served as consultant on worship for Agricultural Missions, Inc., who published a series of quarterly bulletins containing such materials. I also wrote five or six of the occasional papers on rural church life and work which were published by the organization.

In addition to considerable writing in this field, I had the opportunities to teach and lead workshops and seminars in the area of worship. Each year a large group of missionaries on furlough met at Warren Wilson College at Swannanoa in the North Carolina mountains for several weeks of intensive in-service education. The format was to concentrate on one major topic for a week. In July 1944, I spent a week with a group of eighty missionaries, centering on worship in rural churches. The preceding week the leader was Dr. Frank Laubach. We overlapped being there on Sunday evening. He preached in the vesper service in the rustic log chapel of the college. After the service he and I sat for hours on the quiet moonlit hillside, talking. Having him share his experiences in prayer was a profound spiritual treat. At one point near the end of our conversation, he put his hand on mine and said quietly, "Brother Ziegler, I have been praying for you every minute we have been talking!"

In the summer of 1950, I was one of the instructors in the summer school at Candler School of Theology of Emory University in Atlanta for a three week period. The group of over a hundred rural ministers included the "Rural Pastor of the Year" from each of fifteen southern states, who received scholarships from the *Progressive Farmer,* the widely-read farm periodical for the South. A fellow instructor and roommate was Dr. Arthur Raper, a famous rural sociologist and author of "Tenants of the Almighty," one of the books which gave a most revealing picture of southern rural communities. On each of the two weekends, I went home with one of the state rural pastors. The first weekend, July 9, I was with the Georgia pastor, A. Jack Waldrep, who took me to his rural parish in the mountains of northern Georgia. The next weekend I spent with Robert Glenn, a Disciples pastor at Valhermosa Springs, Alabama. Here I preached in a new church, built by the local people, of colorful sandstone and walled and sealed inside with fragrant red cedar.

Deane Edwards, the scholarly executive of the Federal Council's Commission on Worship, frequently called upon me to share leadership in two-day worship seminars in various parts of the country. Usually these would include a great choir festival, led by my lifelong colleague and friend, Alvin Frantz Brightbill, of the Bethany Seminary faculty. We held such seminars in Beloit and Barraboo, Wisconsin; Naperville, Illinois; Columbus, Ohio; Elmira, New York; and York, Pennsylvania. After the Federal Council was absorbed into the new National Council of Churches in 1951, Dr. Edwards served for many years as secretary of the Hymn Society of America.

The growing intense interest all over America in strengthening rural churches and in deepening their corporate worship, led to my having many invitations to speak in theological seminaries and the annual Town and Country Church Convocations. In three of these latter gatherings it was my privilege to lead the worship sessions.

In July 1948, Agricultural Missions, Inc. selected and sent to a two-week workshop on worship a group of fifteen missionaries and national church leaders, at Bridgewater. I directed this workshop, and through it formed lasting friendships with some very wonderful and dedicated people. There were persons there who were missionaries or national church leaders from China, India, the Philippines, Argentina, Chile and several African countries.

All this ecumenical activity did not preclude responsible involvement in the larger areas of the Church of the Brethren. I served on the District Board of the Second Virginia District while at Bridgewater, and as moderator of the 1951 District Conference. In 1948, I was elected to the General Brotherhood Board of the Church of the Brethren in the second year of the Board's existence, serving on the Foreign Missions Commission. Across the next twenty years, I served at various times a total of thirteen years on the Board, for two years as chairman of the Foreign Missions Commission.

An interesting evolution of the Church of the Brethren has occurred in the area of evangelism. In my earlier years it was assumed that persons made their decisions to become Christians and unite with the church almost entirely in the context of revivals, or "series of meetings." Preachers who were especially skilled in evangelistic preaching were in great demand. In the period of my years in the ministry, there have been great changes in method, and in some periods almost total abandonment of any serious emphasis upon evangelism, if not hostility to it. Change in emphasis has brought needed change in terminology. Periods of intensive emphasis came to be called preaching missions or spiritual emphasis weeks. I have conducted many such missions, sometimes as intensive evangelistic meetings, more often in the later years using the new terminology.

During the busy and fruitful years from our return to America in 1939 to the conclusion of my pastorate at Bridgewater, I preached in about eighteen of such missions. Though there was a modest number of commitments to Christ directly in these meetings, I hoped for results more solid than a number of accessions to the church. It was my goal to make these missions times of teaching and of lasting inspiration to the churches as well. It was my hope that the preaching and teaching ministry of these missions would be of enough permanent inspirational value to congregations in which I was the evangelist, that mere numbers of accessions would not be the measure of the effectiveness of my work.

During these extremely busy eleven years I preached over a thousand sermons, averaging over one hundred a year. Over half of them were in the two large churches of which I was pastor for nine years, the others in many other churches, both Brethren and non-Brethren, in conferences, preaching missions, college and seminary chapels, and ecumenical gatherings. I also gave hundreds of lectures or talks, radio broadcasts, and courses in camps, colleges and various kinds of workshops or seminars.

As I look at this record, I see more clearly than ever why the churches I served as pastor sometimes became concerned that I was away from home and the home church too much! My health was usually good, though I did have four brief periods of hospitalization during the first six years of this time. I found that what St. Paul wrote about strength being made perfect in weakness, and being able to do all things through Christ who strengthens, was true for me, too. Through these years, Ilda's health remained remarkably stable, especially after the birth of our son, Donald. Both of us came into the fifties unafraid, mature, and most grateful for God's continued sustaining mercy and unmistakable guidance.

An event which gave me deep satisfaction and humility, near the end of this decade, was Bethany Seminary's award of the honorary Doctor of Divinity degree. Dr. Warren W. Slabaugh read the citation which was warm and dignified, yet spoke of the appreciation of the seminary community for my work as missionary, preacher, and author. I had also been elected to the Board of Directors of the Seminary in 1947 and served a five-year term. In 1950, I served on Standing Committee of Annual Conference held in Grand Rapids, Michigan, and was reading clerk of the conference.

Later in the year, there was a great ecumenical event in Cleveland, Ohio, when the Federal Council of Churches and seven other national ecumenical organizations united to form the new National Council of Churches in the United States. Though not a delegate, because of my years of involvement with several of these organizations the Bridgewater Church permitted me to go as a guest to this impressive event. One of my sharpest memories of the convocation has an unpleasant taste. J. Howard Pew, the rich conservative Presbyterian president of the Sun Oil Company, made a long and boring speech urging that the new council follow the conservative, cautious path which he and other rich layman could support!

CHAPTER 8

Come Over to Macedonia!

*I*n late summer of 1950, Raymond R. Peters, who was the first secretary of the Church of the Brethren General Brotherhood Board, interviewed me for a new position on the denomination's national staff. He told me that the Board was deeply concerned about the growth of the church and wished to establish a new staff position which would be chiefly in evangelism, but also carry the portfolio of rural church concerns. M. R. Zigler, who had cared for rural church matters was now directing our European program. Raymond strongly urged that I consider taking this assignment. It was a difficult choice. I had been at Bridgewater three years, and the pastorate was challenging and productive. Yet the offer looked very attractive. I was deeply interested in both of these important areas and was already serving on the Board, so I knew the background of the offer. At first I was much inclined to say no. Even though I would have nearly a year to finish my pastoral work at Bridgewater, I felt it was a mistake to leave so soon. I talked with a number of trusted friends in the church and elsewhere and Ilda and I made it a matter of long and honest thought and prayer. The decision to accept the new position did not come as an easy or spectacularly inspired call, but we decided finally that the opportunity to work at a denomination-wide ministry should take precedence, and we said yes.

We told the Bridgewater church board of our decision late in autumn, planning to terminate our pastorate in June 1951. In November, Ilda and I went to the General Brotherhood Board meeting and took time to look for a place to live. We bought a large frame house about fifty years old, at 28 South Edison Avenue, in Elgin, Illinois. The owners stayed in the house until we were ready to move in on June 1. The house was on a quiet street, and there was a huge old Bing cherry tree in the back yard and beautiful maples in the front. Good schools for the children were close by. The Highland Avenue Church of the Brethren was within easy walking distance. Several of my Elgin cousins, and some close friends, the Brightbills and Leland Brubakers, lived close by. The Brethren Service truck moved our considerable accumulation of household goods early in June of 1951.

Annual Conference was to be in San Jose, California, and as a staff member I was expected to attend. This gave an opportunity, too, for a good and much-needed vacation trip. After ten days in my new office, our family started for the West Coast. It was a great trip! We stopped at Grand Canyon on our way west. While I was busy with Board meetings in San Jose before Conference began, my son, Bob, who did much of the driving, took the family to Sequoia and Kings Canyon National Parks. On the way home we saw Yellowstone Park also. While we were at Grand Canyon, Bob and I planned to hike some little way down the Bright Angel trail into the canyon before breakfast. We left at dawn; the trail was good, and the sunrise colors were superb. When we had gone some distance we were quite thirsty and decided to go on to Indian Springs, which we could see a short way below us. There we had a refreshing drink, rested, watched a herd of friendly mule deer, then started back up the trail. We didn't realize that we had come down about three thousand feet! By the time we neared the top, it was long past breakfast time! I have rarely been so exhausted.

Desmond Bittinger was moderator of Conference that year. He is a gentle and peaceable man, and a popular preacher. He had served six years as editor of the *Gospel Messenger,* and had now begun a long term as president of McPherson College. Perhaps his greatest fault as moderator was his constant striving to keep all proceedings totally peaceful!

Two incidents stand out in my memory of that conference. One was told me by Desmond Bittinger. It seems that since there is no Church of the Brethren near San Jose, the Brethren were an unknown quantity. The Chamber of Commerce, eager to make the Brethren welcome, researched our history, and found that the church was of German origin. They assumed that all Germans drink a lot of beer, so they advised all taverns and liquor stores to stock up heavily on beer! It may have been after this conference that some business men remarked ruefully that the Brethren came to town with a ten-dollar bill in one hand and the Ten Commandments in the other, determined not to break either!

The other incident vivid in my memory was meeting J. Calvin Bright, who just arrived home the day Conference began, from China, where he had been detained in a Chinese prison for over a year. He was weak and emaciated and, seated in a chair, he gave a moving account of his last years in China and this prison ordeal.

Upon our return from the conference, we settled into our new home, and Bob and Connie moved to Bethany Theological Seminary in Chicago, where Bob planned to work for the master's degree in religious education. We had looked forward to harvesting bushels of luscious Bing cherries from our big tree. But the cherries ripened while we were in California, birds and neighborhood children ate most of them, and a windstorm blew a third of the tree down. When I cut up the fallen limb, I found ten fine cherries. We had paid five dollars to have the tree sprayed, so our cherries cost us fifty cents each!

The mile walk to the Brethren offices on South State Street was really exhilarating and I usually walked. My new office was between Charles Zunkel's Home Mission office on one side and the press room on the other. During most of my working hours the thunder and vibration of the big printing presses served as accompaniment to my conversations and my studies. I was assigned a competent young secretary, Estelle Ball, who worked in my office most of my four years on the staff. Charles Zunkel, who was Ministry and Home Missions secretary, was my senior colleague, and we worked together happily.

As Charles, Raymond Peters and I discussed plans for my work, it seemed good to spend about forty percent of my time, at least, in field work. Office time would be spent planning, writing, and in consultation with other staff persons. My task was to stimulate the total church to be evangelistic, and to help the church to discover and use new methods of witness. About one-fourth of my time would be given to rural church concerns. I would have many opportunities to speak in district and regional conferences, and in local churches or groups of churches.

Since the Church of the Brethren was fully committed to cooperative ministries wherever possible, I worked closely with the Department of Evangelism and the Town and Country Church Commission of the National Council of Churches, and with Agricultural Missions, Inc. Membership in these departments was an invaluable learning opportunity for me. In the Department of Evangelism, I worked closely with my counterparts from many other denominations, and with Dr. Jesse Bader, the "Mr. Evangelism" of the National Council of Churches, and Dr. Harry Kalas, who headed up the National Christian Teaching Missions. I learned much from these two leaders, and from such creative prophets as Harry Denman of the Methodist Church, Elmer Homrighausen of Princeton and George Sweazey of the Presbyterian Church. The time seemed ripe for a great forward move in evangelism, and the meetings of the commission were full of excitement and hope. On one occasion, Dr. Bader introduced to the commission a young Princeton graduate, Warren Ost, who had an exciting plan for a Christian ministry in the National Parks. The commission adopted the plan and sponsored the ministry with Ost as its director. This ministry, now independent of the National Council of Churches, has done incalculable service, and thousands of college and seminary students have had the doors opened to significant summers of service.

The need for the kind of ministry I would bring to the Church of the Brethren was well expressed by Rufus P. Bucher, an old friend to me, and to my father and grandfather before me, a popular and effective evangelistic preacher. At the 1951 Conference, he said to me in his rich Pennsylvania Dutch accent, "Brother Edward, I'm glad you will be giving our church help in new ways of sharing the Gospel. Sometimes now, I preach in an evangelistic meeting to a great congregation packing the meetinghouse, and when I give the invitation, nobody comes forward. Then the pastor says to comfort me, 'Brother Bucher, there chust weren't any sinners here tonight except those already on the deacon body of the church!'"

The years on the denominational staff were strenuous but rewarding. Travelling about fifty thousand miles a year, I spoke and taught in most of the districts and in more than four hundred churches. The congregations were most receptive to the new emphasis in evangelism. In several areas we set up new patterns of preaching missions, involving many laymen. In these missions there was less prima donna preaching and no high pressure "altar calls." The rising tide of interest in evangelism, and the enthusiastic response of most churches and pastors to the new approaches which we tried and commended, bore fruit in a marked increase across the Brotherhood in baptisms and church growth. During three of these years, there was greater increase in church membership than in any of the previous twenty years, and probably in any year since then. I strongly emphasized adequate training for church membership, and prompt absorption of all new members into the life and ministries of the congregation.

Charles Zunkel and I shared deep concern for the ministry of the church. He and I agreed that we had not left the pastoral ministry; we were pastors to pastors, in a specialized form of enabling ministry. I had a number of opportunities during these busy years to install pastors and to preach at the dedication of new church buildings.

Because of my staff position, I had considerable responsibility at Annual Conference, setting up, planning, and sometimes leading sectional meetings on evangelism or rural church concerns. For a few years we set up a plan to select a "Rural Brethren Minister of the Year," and honored him at Conference. In 1952, I was elected as assistant moderator of the Conference. It was held that year in Richmond, Virginia. It was expected that the assistant moderator be parliamentarian, and preside when the moderator asked him to do so. Since the moderator was my former teacher, Dr. Ralph W. Schlosser, I thought he would need no help on parliamentary procedure. Even though business sessions were long, arduous, and at times tense, Dr. Schlosser at no point asked for my help. He became quite fatigued and really needed relief, but would not ask for it. I was about as useful as traditional vice presidents are.

President Paul Robinson of Bethany Seminary felt that seminary students needed the emphasis which was being promoted in the church at large. He arranged with Secretary Peters and the General Brotherhood Board for me to teach one quarter of each year in the seminary. So in the spring quarter I taught a class in evangelism, and one on Rural Sociology, alternating with Rural Church Program and Ministry. There were few district conferences in spring, so I would use half-time in this exciting program. I commuted four mornings a week from Elgin to Chicago for this work. Through my field work and teaching in the seminary, I came to know almost all of the pastors and leaders in the Church of the Brethren over a period of several years.

I found that the National Christian Teaching Missions, originally designed and led by Dr. Harry Kalas, made a great deal of sense as comprehensive community approaches to evangelism. The missions consisted of a series of seminars for pastors and a community religious survey, which was very carefully planned, and followed up by visitation ministries carried on by local congregations. The approach to people was characterized as fellowship evangelism. After receiving training for leading these missions I had the great satisfaction of leading several, in widely-separated areas of the country, under the auspices of the National Council of Churches. Three which were especially successful were in Pomona, California for Pomona, Claremont and LaVerne; Lansing, Michigan; and in York County, Pennsylvania. After leaving Elgin, I led two others, in Northern Rockingham County, Virginia, and in Clarksburg, West Virginia. During this time, I also gave lectures in a number of theological seminaries, usually on the Rural Church and Worship.

An example of a busy itinerary on one of my Brotherhood trips was this:

March 5-9 (1952), five addresses to the Pacific Regional Conference at La-Verne, California.

March 10-12, addresses in Whittier, Glendale, Panorama City, and Fresno, California.

March 13-14, two addresses in Berkeley Baptist Divinity School, California, and one address in San Francisco.

March 15, Train to San Diego, bridge out, bus two hundred miles to Los Angeles, four hours sleep on a station bench.

March 16, Train to San Diego, preached dedication sermon, flew back to San Francisco, slept five hours in the airport lounge.

March 17, five-hour flight through a wild storm to Eugene, Oregon.

March 17-19, Ministers' Retreat at Springfield, Oregon.

March 21-23, Addresses in churches at Myrtle Point, Albany and Weston, Oregon.

March 24, Flight from Walla Walla, Washington to Chicago and home!

March 25-28, four lectures at Bethany Seminary!

In that one month, I travelled well over six thousand miles, and spoke at least twenty-five times. Not many months were so crowded, fortunately.

Brethren Volunteer Service, beginning in 1948, had captured the imagination of hundreds of Brethren youth and was the channel through which some of the most idealistic young persons were brought into life-long ministries in the church. It seemed to me that some, especially college students, might be channelled into summer church service. In consultation with Charles Zunkel, and Youth Director Ed Crill, we worked out a plan of summer service. For each of three summers, we recruited ten to fourteen good students, who received two weeks of training, then went out in teams of two to selected churches. We held the first training session in the Martinsburg Church, Pennsylvania; the second in the Bridgewater Church, Virginia, and the third in Camp Sugar Grove in Southern Ohio. These were intensive training sessions, giving me a good opportunity to pair students and match them with churches. Following the training, they worked mostly in smaller churches, conducting Vacation Schools, working with youth groups, camp leaders, preaching, even conducting evangelistic meetings. They sent in reports each week and a final summer's report. The churches they served provided room and board and a modest salary, which helped out with college costs. Reports from the churches were quite enthusiastic as well. In planning and preparation, I had studied the plan of the Mormon Church in sending out their young people as missionaries, and had corresponded with the president of that church.

The young people had many good stories to tell of their experiences. Perhaps none was more exciting than the story of one of the last evenings at Camp Sugar Grove. They planned a vesper service on a hill in a pasture just across the road from the old church. I was a bit concerned, for there was a herd of big Shorthorn steers grazing there. But one of the boys, whose home was nearby, assured us these cattle were gentle and harmless. However, soon after we were seated on our blankets and started singing, the steers surrounded us in a ring, curious about us. We weren't alarmed, until a huge white-faced bull came marching purposefully up the hill. He pushed through the herd of lesser cattle, pawing and snorting. I suggested we get up and walk—not run!—to the fence. We were singing "Christian Let Your Burning Light" and as the girls started down the hill, the boys and I warily followed, all of us singing, "Keep up courage, never fail/Till you're safe within the vale!"

I believe we had initiated a plan of summer service that could be of great value both to the students and to the church. Brethren Volunteer Service for the most part spread out into many areas of service and lost some of the evangelistic emphasis which I thought would be a very valuable aspect of it.

Much has been written about the shallowness and weaknesses of the popular evangelistic "crusades" and the church extension methods of the

1950s, and many of the criticisms have been just. I believe that the emphasis we followed and the kind of evangelism we promoted during four years in this office were sound, biblical and of much promise. But by the time I left the office in 1955, a significant segment of the leadership in the Church of the Brethren tended to de-emphasize evangelism, or so to broaden it that it had little of the witnessing, discipling qualities which alone can "win men to Christ." I feel that at the same time the Church of the Brethren turned away from another important part of our church's mission. We had been predominantly a rural denomination, with some strong churches in a few urban centers. But in the 50s and 60s, we began to put most of our resources into getting into the cities and suburbs, and developing so-called "community" churches. Some leaders felt that there was little hope for the survival of the small rural church. We tended to let the evangelism and religious nurture of rural people go by default to the Southern Baptists and Penecostal or independent churches. If anyone in the whole spectrum of American church life could maintain strong rural churches, we should have! It has seemed to me that we have tried so hard to emerge from our sectarian, rural background, and become an elite partner of the mainline Protestant bodies that we have come periously close to denying our heritage and losing our soul. And we have continued until today to lose ground in rural America, and have not been conspicuously successful as an urban denomination. Surely our church has an important part to play in the redemption of the city and the suburbs. But "this ought ye have done and not let the other undone!"

A good start toward remedying this situation is in the innovative program for training leadership for small churches, sponsored jointly by the Parish Ministries Commission of the General Board of the church and Bethany Theological Seminary. The first two years of this program, entitled "Education for a Shared Ministry," were financed by a grant from the Lilly Foundation. In this program, leaders from the congregation are given training, so they can be in the tradition of the "free ministry," but with guidance and intensive training from the program. This has much promise for the renewal and strengthening of small rural churches.

Though Ilda never complained, she carried far more than her share of family responsibility. Her diabetic condition continued to deteriorate, and far too often for our peace of mind she suffered severe insulin shock. Most sobering to me was the day when I came home from a trip to find that she was in the hospital recovering from an especially severe shock. I was away from home too much and knew that I must change positions so that I could stay closer to her and the children.

In the spring of 1955 I was offered a pastorate again, and also a full-time teaching position in Bethany Seminary. I chose the pastorate and was called to the growing Williamson Road Church, in Roanoke, Virginia. Former Bridgewater College friends, Dr. Frank Strickler, and his wife Sylvia, were active in the church there, and he was the prime mover in our receiving the call. The church was only seven years old, was building a parsonage and was starting a good sanctuary building. A college friend, Carson Key, was the founding pastor of the church, and it was already a strong congregation with about two hundred members. At the end of the summer of 1955, we moved to Roanoke and began what was to be my longest and one of my happiest pastorates.

Returning to the pastorate was a good move. The Williamson Road Church was a strong, growing church, with great potential. The first unit of the church building was impressive but incomplete. Work had already begin on completion of a beautiful and commodious sanctuary, shortly before our arrival. The parsonage was by far the most comfortable and convenient home we had ever lived in. We hoped that there would be no other move for many years. The children were soon in excellent schools. Roanoke is a beautiful city nestled in a wide elbow between the Blue Ridge Mountains and the timbered ridges of the Alleghenies to the west and north. The Roanoke River flowed through Roanoke and broke through the ranges of the Blue Ridge nearby on its way to the Atlantic. I have always loved mountains, and there we were closely surrounded by them. Not far away, we could drive on the Blue Ridge Parkway, the lovely scenic drive along the crest of the Blue Ridge which soon would extend all the way to the Great Smokies.

A year later, the new sanctuary was completed. It was good to have Raymond Peters come to be the dedication speaker, not only because he was a life-long friend and colleague, but because his father and mother lived there. His father, J. Bunyan Peters, was the greatly loved moderator of the congregation. About the same time, we dedicated a new Allen organ, which was capable of producing magnificent organ tones that filled our new meetinghouse with glorious sound. Our friend, Ruth Weybright, from Bridgewater College, gave a fine organ recital when we dedicated the organ. We had a good choir, and the services of worship were deeply appreciated and called forth my own greatest skills in planning and leading, and in preaching.

Here in Roanoke the Church of the Brethren was one of the larger denominations. As in most southern communities, half of the Christians were Baptists! The Methodists were second in number, and the Brethren, Episcopalians and Presbyterians were approximately equal in third place. There were now five strong Brethren congregations in the city and a dozen more within twelve miles! Since Baptists would have nothing to do with councils of churches, the ecumenical movement here was channeled into a strong ministers' conference. Brethren ministers participated fully in this organization, and several had served as president of it. I served one year as chairman of its program committee. The conference brought many renowned speakers to our community. A wealthy and pious old merchant of the community each year invited all the ministers and their wives to have a sumptuous dinner, with an inspiring speaker, at White

Sulphur Springs, West Virginia, or at Natural Bridge, both of them beautiful resorts not far from Roanoke.

We loved Roanoke and found the people at Williamson Road friendly, congenial, and eager to grow. We found there a certain courteous gentility, which seemed characteristic of southern Virginia people. I found less tensions or cliques there than in any other church I have served in, before or since then.

Ilda's health remained fairly good during our Roanoke years. She sang alto in the church choir and gave much leadership in children's Christian nurture. One of her greatest achievements there was starting a kindergarten in the church and training others to share in teaching it. She continued it as long as we lived in Roanoke.

Our younger children were rapidly growing up in these years in Roanoke. Donald entered Bridgewater College in 1959, to major in art. In this same year he was licensed to the ministry. Ruth Ann specialized in science in high school, participating several times in National Science Fairs, with a fascinating study in flat-worm memory training. A good spiritual experience for her was going to National Youth Conference in Lake Junaluska, North Carolina, in the summer of 1958.

Many invitations to speak at conferences, especially district and regional conferences, and at seminaries and universities came to me those days, because of my work in evangelism and in rural church concerns. One of those occasions which gave me much satisfaction was preaching at Montreat, North Carolina, to the Georgia Synod of the Presbyterian Church. I was asked to preach on a theme I had used in the lectures I had given earlier at Columbia Theological Seminary on "Buying a Farm at Anathoth."

I had based this sermon on the account in Jeremiah 32 of the prophet's purchase of his cousin's fields at Anathoth, while the country was overrun by the Chaldean armies and Jerusalem was about to fall.

The story of the prophet Jeremiah's purchase of his ancestral fields is a superb illustration how the man of God speaks for hope . . .

When the deepest despairing gloom had settled over the people, Jeremiah did a strange, unbelievable thing. His cousin Hanamel, at grave risk, made his way into Jerusalem from their home village of Anathoth, three miles to the northeast, on a shelf of the central plateau, looking off over the great Jordan river-trench. He hunted out Jeremiah where he was confined in the guard's court, and offered to sell him his land. The fields, formerly owned by Jeremiah's Uncle Shallum, were now worthless, overrun by and indeed in the possession of the Chaldeans at that moment. Of all times and places to buy land, this was the most unlikely!

But the Word of the Lord came to Jeremiah to buy it. Agreeing on a price of seventeen silver shekels, the cousins wrote a bill of sale and a deed to the land, and went through all the necessary formalities of transfer. How the magistrates and bankers laughed. What would this crazy fool of an old prophet do next? This was as silly as buying the bottom of a salt marsh.

But God had a purpose which Jeremiah boldly and happily announced. No one knew better than the prophet did the imminence of defeat, disaster and destruction. He had seen the danger and the final tragedy long before anyone else had. And yet, he found that God had plans on beyond the dark gateways of this national calamity. So by this courageous and strange purchase of land, Jeremiah made the bold and glorious prophecy that God would sometime restore his people to their homeland. Beyond tragedy was Hope. . . .

In many rural areas, there is a mood of hopelessness and defeat. The mechanizing of agriculture, the wearing out of the land, the lure of high-paying jobs in the city have decimated the population of many rural communities. Population is shifting at a terrific rate. As the people thin out, many churches, lacking creative leadership, have become mortally sick, and in the last twenty-five years, more than twenty-five thousand have closed their doors. The schools consolidate, leaving no real center of neighborhood or community life. As the resources of top soil are depleted by careless land use and erosion, a more serious human erosion destroys the very community itself.

Those who are left in the community often have a sense of inferiority about themselves, their work, community and its institutions. . . .

As a rural pastor in a community you will see change and decay. When other institutions fade out, fold up, and flee, let the church and the minister stand like rock. Let them say, "It is God's will that the church abide. Nothing can dismay us or make us afraid. Buy your farm at Anathoth!"

So we are to stake out a claim for God. We are to declare His unchanging purposes, his eternal goodness, his great lovingkindness, his compassionate concern for his family. We will stake out our claim in true faith and invincible hope, for we know that we build with God . . .

So buy your farm at Anathoth! Dig deep into the soil and put down your roots. Stay with it. Speak out for hope, for God, for His Kingdom. It is yours to say, when men's hearts quail in fear, when personal tragedy grips them, when the twilight of atomic night threatens, when all around is change and loss of hope—"God Still Reigns!" The Kingdom of the world is become the Kingdom of our Lord and of his Christ, and he shall reign forever and ever. Hallelujah!

I continued to be heavily involved in the district and Brotherhood programs. In 1956, I was elected again to the General Brotherhood Board. For a year or two I served on the Education Commission. Then I went back again to the area of my first concern, the Foreign Missions Commission. I represented the First District of Virginia on Standing Committee in 1959 at the Ocean Grove Conference. At that time the General Brotherhood Board and Standing Committee met on the Sunday morning before Conference for worship, and I preached the sermon.

For a number of years, the moderators of Annual Conference were almost always college or seminary administrators. Actually, since 1925, only four pastors had served as moderator. At the 1959 conference, there was a strong feeling that a pastor should be elected, and I was elected to this responsible office. Significantly, since then about half of the moderators have been pastors, and four laymen have served. I have no doubt that in the near future some of the very able women in the church will also serve in this post.

An almost amusing sequence of moderators followed: Charles Zunkel, Nevin Zuck, and Harry K. Zeller—four Z's in a row! As William Beahm, who preceded me as moderator remarked, "Conference is now scraping the bottom of the barrel—alphabetically!"

During my year as moderator, the Williamson Road Church was most supportive and seemed glad to have their pastor in demand as a speaker in district and regional conferences and preaching missions. I can truthfully say that I thoroughly enjoyed presiding at the Annual Conference, which was held June 14-19, 1960, on the campus of the University of Illinois at Urbana. My "moderator's address" was on the theme, "Called to Break Bread Together." As moderator I sought to be a reconciler, for the newly founded Brethren Revival Fellowship was making strong overtures to bring the church back to a more conservative stance, and to have the church withdraw membership in the councils of churches. While I took a strong stand for ecumenical cooperation, I tried also to have Standing Committee and Conference hear the concerns of the Brethren Revival Fellowship and assure them they were accepted and loved. At Standing Committee's suggestion, the conference passed a strong resolution of support for the National and World Councils. I was elected as one of our two representatives to the World Council of Churches, along with Norman J. Baugher, who was General Secretary of the General Brotherhood Board. Charles Zunkel, who had been my colleague on the Brotherhood staff, gave me invaluable assistance and support during the conference, and I was happy to pass the gavel on to him as the next moderator.

The Williamson Road Church experienced steady growth during my six years there as pastor. I baptized seventy persons, and we received one hundred ninety-three new members including those baptized. Only ten members of the church died. I never felt that I was very strong in pastoral counselling. Yet some of my most successful personal work was done during these years. A heartwarming finale to a long series of counselling sessions came in this way: A fine young couple with an attractive five-year-old son had a beautiful home, and all that money could bring them. But their marriage deteriorated and finally there was a bitter separation. After many sessions with me, they decided to start over. When we had the preparation service for our Love Feast, the couple came forward to reconsecrate their lives and renew their marriage vows. The warmth and joy of the congregation was beautiful and genuine. I had never heard a word of gossip or condemnation in the congregation, and the marriage was back on a solid Christian basis with the total trust and love of the community of faith.

In Roanoke I was happily involved in the religious life of the community. One year I organized for the Ministers' Conference a religious survey of the city and county, which collected data on more than forty thousand family units. Our church was also involved in the resettling of about forty Hungarian refugees, and in a massive drive to collect clothing for relief, when over ten tons of good quality garments were sent to Church World Service.

We hoped to have a long ministry in Roanoke. There were some influential members of the church who were dubious by my serving on the World Council of Churches, especially since it involved a trip to India in the fall of 1961 to attend the Third Assembly in New Delhi. It was the hope of the Foreign Missions Commission that on that trip I could visit our Indian churches. The pastoral board of the church was reluctant to grant several months for this trip and thought that my rather modest salary should not be increased because of the trip. So in early 1961, I resigned as pastor, in the hope that I could serve in a congregation which would be more accepting of my continued involvement in the larger church. Nevertheless, I look back upon the six years in the pastorate in Roanoke as a most fruitful and happy period in my ministry, and I have the warmest feelings of appreciation and gratitude for the wonderful congregation there. Since that time the Williamson Road Church has become the strongest of the six Churches of the Brethren in Roanoke, and has provided a second Annual Conference moderator in Ira B. Peters, a quiet, dedicated layman, who has been one of the strongest lay leaders in the local church and district.

CHAPTER 9

From Virginia to California Via India

*S*oon after my resignation from the Williamson Road pastorate was accepted, I was invited to come to the Oakton Church in Eastern Virginia, just fifteen miles from Washington, to be a candidate for the pastorate there. I told the Oakton Board of my plans to visit India in the fall, for the World Council of Churches Assembly, and they assured me that the church would be fully supportive of my going. Not only that, they would gladly continue my salary through the six weeks of my absence. The salary seemed attractive, considerably above what I had been receiving. With the prospect of soon having two children in college, the increase was welcome. I preached my last sermon at Williamson Road on August 27, and the next Sunday my first at Oakton.

The Oakton Church had been started about sixty years earlier by a group of Brethren farmers from the Valley of Virginia who thought the proximity to Washington would ensure a good market for milk and farm produce. They were right—for a while. But by 1961, when the urban sprawl had made Fairfax County one of the fastest growing areas in the nation, we had only one active farmer left in the large congregation—and his farm was fourteen miles from the church! The makeup of the congregation was quite diverse, with many members from all parts of the country who came to the area to work in government and the special industries that surrounded the Capitol. The membership was over five hundred, and the church building was both commodious and beautiful.

At Oakton, for the first time in my years as a pastor, I had a nearly full time secretary, in the person of Louise Denham Bowman, who later became an active leader in the women's movement in the Church of the Brethren. For some years now she has carried much responsibility on the staff of the denomination's Washington office.

It had been our plan that Ilda would go with me on the trip to India. But in January of 1961, major surgery for me and a costly hospital stay exhausted the funds we had saved, so we could not afford the expense of her going. Her staying behind was the greatest disappointment of this memorable trip.

I flew by the most direct route possible, leaving Washington on October 26, 1961, and arriving in the steamy October heat of Bombay on Saturday morning, the 28th. For the first time I knew the meaning of jet lag! Jack McCray, our missionary in Bombay, met me, and I had my first view of the immense changes which had come to this huge, busy, poverty-smitten metropolis in the twenty-two years since I had left India.

On Sunday morning, the 29th, I went by train to Dahanu Road to begin my three week visit to the area of India I had come to love so well a generation earlier. I preached that morning in the little church in Gujarati, and again in the evening. Although I had tried to brush up my knowledge of the language, it was slow going at first. The congregation was very attentive and helpful. When I halted, searching for a word, three or four persons would call out a word — not always the same. During the day, I talked with the student nurses, several of them daughters of my fellow workers years before.

The next day, I went by train to Vyara, where we had spent so many good years. On the way I indiscreetly bought and ate some delicious Indian sweets. In the next five days, Everett Fasnacht took me all over the Vyara area and to Ahwa in the Dangs Forest, by jeep! By the end of my first day there, I found I had almost total recall of the language and preached fourteen times in five days. By the time we reached Ahwa, however, my foolish indulgence in sweets had brought on a severe attack of gastro-enteritis. Dr. Wampler and Glen Campbell drove out from Bulsar the next day and took me back to the hospital where I had three days of quiet rest.

During the next two weeks, I visited the rest of our mission stations and Ahmedabad, the state capital. Here I spoke to the students in the United States School of Theology and preached once more in the large Presbyterian Church. I closed my visit in Gujarat leading a retreat for all the Brethren ministers at the beautiful Broach retreat center, high on a bluff above the broad Narbudda River. During the nineteen days of my visit, I preached forty-one times, in the vernacular! The welcome from the many people with whom we had worked during our missionary term was overwhelming!

I was tremendously moved and impressed by the vigor and vision of the Indian Church. Many of the Indian Christian leaders would compare very favorably with their American counterparts. I found many lay men and women who were able and trusted workers in the professions, especially in the healing arts, and in government service and business; they also were strong supporters of the church.

I was deeply impressed with the economic improvement of the Christian community. In the Vyara area, the construction of a dam on the Tapti River was providing irrigation water, and many Christian farmers were now prospering. When I was there, a trainload of bananas was being shipped every day from the area! Near Anklesvar, oil had been discovered. But most important of all, the years of aid given by the rural reconstruction centers, and the resourceful *gram sevaks,* (servants of the villages) had given an immense boost to the economy of the whole region.

It appeared to me that the mission to India had laid enduring foundations, and that the Indian Church was mature, strong, and growing. The Christian community which the Brethren had started in India no longer felt dependent on the church in America. They longed for continued strong cooperation, but not on a paternalistic basis. Conversations with many leaders indicated that they wished to continue deep friendships with fellow Christians in the American church. Mission could only be a two-way road. By that time, the church was actively sharing in negotiations which were to lead to the formation of the Church of North India. Indian Brethren were taking strong leadership in the movement; when it came into being, a Brethren man, Ishwarlal V. Christachari, became the first Bishop of Gujarat.

I spent several days in an excellent youth camp at the seaside near Bulsar. The issues these bright, serious Indian youth were discussing marked a responsible younger sector in the church. Hearing an attractive young woman high school teacher discussing Christian ideals of sex and marriage with dignity and candor was refreshing!

When I reached India, I was given a copy of the current issue of *Ajavaliu*, the little newspaper I had started, now still going strong. It contained some special reference to my visit. It was good to see its quality of endurance as a voice for the Christian villager's everyday concerns and faith.

I flew to New Delhi for the World Council Assembly. I was one of six Brethren present. M. R. Zigler, who had so long been a stimulating Brethren presence in the Council, was there as a consultant. Norman Baugher, my colleague as a delegate, was there with his wife, Ruth. Kurtis Naylor, our European representative, was a guest and was my roommate in the old Imperial Hotel. Shantilal Bhagat was there as an observer from the Indian Church. And Norman Ford, a veteran Young Men's Christian Association worker in India and a Brethren minister was present part of the time.

It was a daring venture for the World Council of Churches to meet in the timeless yet ultra-modern capital of India, proclaiming boldly its theme, "Jesus Christ, the Light of the World." Perhaps it was presumptuous to proclaim so great a message when all India knew it was the so-called Christian nations which had plunged the world into two devastating wars and had held many underprivileged peoples of the world in centuries of colonial bondage. Yet the Council Assembly was characterized by penitence more than by arrogance; by earnest searching for the will of God for all men rather than by trumpeting achievement and superiority. The Assembly demonstrated the remarkable unity of the church of Christ, yet celebrated its diversity of cultures and ethnic and national roots.

All of the meetings of the Assembly were held in the beautiful new Vigyan Bhavan, which had been built for UNESCO meetings; however, large public meetings were held in a spacious and colorful Shamiana, or colorful flat-roofed Indian tent, nearby. The schedule was a crowded one, with a great opening service in the Shamiana led by Presidents of the Council and with a sermon by an eloquent Burmese pastor. There were daily services of worship in many traditions; periods for Bible study; thoughtful, sometimes profound or fiery addresses in general sessions; well ordered plenary business sessions; and long hours spent in committee sessions, in which all delegates participated. I was a member of a committee which studied ministerial training for the younger churches, and for the series of Bible studies I was in a group of eighty persons led by Martin Niemöller, the celebrated German pacifist leader.

Up to this time my major ecumenical interest had been in the field of missions. A significant action in an early session of the Assembly was the formal merger of the International Missionary Council with the World Council of Churches. This seemed to make mission a central theme of the whole ecumenical movement and greatly strengthened the Council. The growing unity of the world-wide church was visibly emphasized when sixteen new denominations became full members of the Council. These ranged from the Holy Orthodox Church of Russia and three other national Orthodox churches, to two Pentecostal churches in Latin America. Acceptance of the Russian Church, with its fifty million adherents, was a matter of world interest and the occasion of a vicious attack on the Council by Carl McIntyre and his puppet International Council of Christian Churches. McIntyre was present as a press representative, a pathetically bombastic and almost ludicrous figure. He planned a massive demonstration outside Vigyan Bhavan on the day the Russian Church was admitted. About three demonstrators showed up, and even McIntyre himself did not appear with them.

The delegation of fourteen Russian churchmen with their full beards and rich vestments was a colorful group. At first they seemed shy and aloof, but after a few days of warm acceptance they seemed very hungry for fellowship. They bought hundreds of books which had been unavailable in Russia. And they were eager to be in touch with the peace churches. Norman Baugher had a historic meeting with them, which led to the later years of shared discussions between the Brethren and the Russian Orthodox both in Russia and the United States. It seemed significant that the average age of the members of the Russian delegation was thirty-six. Their chairman, Metropolitan Nikodim, thirty-two, was elected one of the presidents of the Council at a later Assembly.

The presidium of six and the central committee of one hundred had a remarkable variety. The new presidium consisted of the scholarly Archbishop of Canterbury, Dr. Michael Ramsey; Sir Francis Ibiam, the fiery Presbyterian governor of Eastern Nigeria; Dr. David Moses, a wise Indian educator; Dr. Martin Niemöller; Charles Parlin, an American Methodist lawyer; and Archbishop Iakovos, the leader of all Greek Orthodox Churches in North America. It seems a serious oversight that there have been only two women presidents of the Council, and only two or three women were elected at this time to the central committee. Though the Church of the Brethren is one of the small denominations in the Council, the esteem in which our witness is held is shown in the service of M. R. Zigler on the central committee from 1953 to 1961, and of Norman Baugher from 1961 to the next Assembly in Uppsala, Sweden, in 1969.

A conspicuous example of Brethren influence was in the debate on an Assembly statement on war. The first statement proposed seemed to many of us much weaker than the Council's firm original statement in 1949 that "all war is sin." In the floor debate, Quakers and a number of eloquent pacifist voices were raised in pleading for a firm and uncompromising position against all war. Baugher and I both spoke. It seemed to us that the Council discounted the Quakers as not so much a church as an idealistic peace society; the other pacifists who spoke, though eloquent, were not really representing the stance of their denominations. We were heard as representatives of a strong and consistent biblically based supporting church. I was invited to meet with the drafting committee to prepare a new and much stronger statement, which was warmly accepted by the Assembly at a later session.

Many facets of this assembly experience remain fresh in my mind as I recall it—the gentle but challenging plea of Prime Minister Jawaharlal Nehru that we do all in our power to influence governments for peace; the almost imperial splendor of a garden party for the whole assembly given by the scholarly vice president of India, Sir Sarvapalli Radhakrishnan in the stately Moghul gardens of the presidential palace; the spirited singing of hymns from many Christian heritages, often sung with great gusto in four or five languages simultaneously; the scandal of our inability to have one Eucharist in which all might join; the hundreds of thousands of pictures taken; the power and eloquent leadership of the scholarly Dutch theologian, Dr. W. A. Visser't Hooft, the secretary of the Council, whose name means "chief fisherman!"

The voices of leaders from the younger churches were strong, wise, persuasive and eloquent in such persons as Daniel T. Niles of Sri Lankha;

Philip Potter of the Caribbean, now general secretary of the Council; Dr. M. M. Thomas of South India; Dr. Takanaka, sharp young Japanese theologian; the spicy Nigerian, Sir Francis Ibiam; and the eloquent evangelist Emilio Castro from Paraguay, were only a few of these strong leaders. In years past, the European Church leaders seemed to have little respect for American theologians. But now, along with administrative genius of men like Franklin Clark Fry and Eugene Carson Blake, the voices of Joseph Sittler and O. Frederick Nolde were heard as mature and theologically oriented American Christian thinkers.

As I returned home in a twenty-hour series of flights, I felt that the participation of the Church of the Brethren in the World Council was right and of great importance. We had so much to learn, so much to share. Though numerically insignificant, we were heard with deep respect. Membership in the Council held no threat, no coercion. Our stance as a peace church, with emphasis on loving service and radical discipleship, was a welcome contribution to the total life of Christ's church in the world. The assembly deepened my faith in the Lord of the church, broadened my vision of Christ as Light of the world, made me more sure than ever of the church's mission and victory. I hoped I could share my vision with the church, beginning at Oakton, and in the denomination. I am sure that my writing and preaching have been deepened and matured by this experience.

Back home again in December 1961, I plunged into my work as pastor. We stayed five years at Oakton. In some respects this was my most difficult period of pastoral ministry. On two main issues we experienced deep tensions and cleavage in the church. One was the race issue. While we had much discussion on it while we were in Roanoke, our church was supportive of my stand for racial justice and integration. At Oakton there was some strong opposition. When I preached my vision of a church inclusive and colorful as a rainbow, on the basis of the biblical nature of the family of God, some members were angered and ceased participation in the church. When I participated in the great "March for Justice" in Washington in August 1963, the wisdom of my going was sharply questioned. Most of the congregation stood with me, but opposition was vocal and bitter.

The other divisive issue was precipitated by our use of new youth curriculum materials published and promoted by the church. Several families were disturbed by the historical-critical approach and thought we should use more fundamentalist materials. There were acrimonious debates, and several families were alienated, leaving the church for more comfortably conservative church homes. On both of these issues I felt that I was torn between trying to win the conservatives in a reconciling ministry and the necessity to be faithful to my vision of justice and faithfulness. I tried to pour oil on the troubled waters, but the oil slick was flammable!

Again at Oakton, I was soon deeply involved in ecumenical affairs.

Elected president of the Fairfax County Council of Churches, I automatically became a member of the board of the Greater Washington Council of Churches. I served two years as vice-president of the Greater Washington Council and learned to know and greatly respect many of the strongest leaders of the church in Washington, such as Dean Francis B. Sayre of the Washington Cathedral, Clarence Cranford and Ed Pruden, pastors of great Baptist churches, David Colwell, Congregational leader, and black leaders who were strong churchmen, such as Walter Washington, Walter Fauntroy, Dr. Josephine Kiles, and many others.

Each year the Council sponsored the strong schools for training leadership in three localities—in Virginia, suburban Maryland, and in the inner city. I taught courses in all three, and also directed in two consecutive years the mission education workshops which drew seven to nine hundred local church workers for an evening and full day of preparation for missionary education in local churches.

Much happened in our personal and family living during the five years in Oakton. Ilda's health seemed to become more precarious, with rather severe glaucoma, and then the beginning of severe congestive heart failure, which several times required hospitalization for a brief period. My own health seemed inexhaustible, but by the end of five years, I felt the need to move to a less demanding pastoral situation where I could care for Ilda better and have her in a more salubrious climate. I still had to be away from home too much, serving again a term on the General Brotherhood Board, on the Fraternal Relations Committee, and heavy district responsibilities.

A rewarding part of my ministry in the Washington area was the opportunity for radio and TV ministry in Washington. For a brief period I had a daily ten-minute program answering questions on faith and life. Continuing the program required sponsors, and before adequate sponsorship was assured, we left the area. There were a satisfying number of phone calls and letters of appreciation for these ministries. In fact, from the time of my York pastorate on, I did a great many radio ministry programs, and in Roanoke, Washington and Bakersfield, California, TV programs.

During the last year at Oakton, I was involved also in the development of Camp Shiloh, ninety miles away in the Blue Ridge Mountains. This is one of the most beautifully located of any church camps, just a few miles below the quiet grandeur of Shenandoah National Park. On one of my early camping weeks there, I helped in erecting stone walls for the main building and set up a self-guiding nature trail. At the present time Camp Shiloh is one of three camps operated by the Mid-Atlantic District, and it has a large acreage of beautiful forest land—over four hundred acres.

During these years at Oakton, Donald graduated from Bridgewater College, then spent two years in Brethren Volunteer Service, most of the time in Bethany Hospital in Chicago. Ruth Ann was married to Warren Baird in June, 1964. He taught in Sandy Spring Friends School in Maryland. She completed her college course at American University, graduating in 1966.

One of the best programs for church renewal developed by the Church of the Brethren was entitled Mission 12. The Oakton Church enthusiastically joined in one of the missions which included three of the Virginia districts. The first main weekend training session was held at Massanetta Springs on January 28-30, 1966. A ferocious blizzard that weekend closed everything, including most roads. Most churches all over the state closed down. With one hundred fifty persons present, we probably had the largest worshipping congregation in Virginia that morning! I did not reach home until Monday noon. Ilda and I had planned to drive to Chicago to bring Donald home from his two years of Volunteer Service that day. Finally on Tuesday we learned that it might be possible to make the trip. We ran into a fresh blizzard in Ohio, but made the trip to Chicago, picked up Donald and all his possessions, went on to Genoa for a night with Jim and Mary Houff, then to Dayton to visit my brother Jesse's. We arrived home on Saturday, and had driven through drifted and icy roads more than eighteen hundred miles in five days! Donald found work nearby and lived at home with us until we left Oakton in late August.

Before Ruth's graduation, we had decided that it was necessary to move. As I noted earlier, I felt that Ilda needed a more congenial climate. And at sixty-three, I felt strongly that I must move to a smaller church which I could serve until the time came for me to retire. When a call came, by telephone and then letters, from the church in Bakersfield, California, it seemed a perfect place to move. I resigned the Oakton pastorate in spring, to take effect in August.

In the meantime, I was invited to spend the autumn quarter as pastor-in-residence at Bethany Theological Seminary. This was a good transition, for we could stop three months en route to California. The last months at Oakton were very busy. The church had experienced slow but steady growth, and the levels of stewardship and participation were high. We were not running away from a difficult situation, but could leave with a sense that it had been a demanding, sometimes heart-wrenching, but also heart-warming five-year ministry!

The three months at Bethany Seminary as pastor-in-residence was a rich and growing experience. After eleven strenuous years in two pastorates, this gave me a breathing space for reflection and renewal. I believe it was a good experience also for the seminary. The program had begun the year before with Raymond Peters as the pastor. We shared fully in the life of the seminary community. I taught a class on Town and Country Church Program, and shared with Paul Robinson in teaching an unpopular course in Church Administration. I also shared in one of the excellent Junior Colloquia, preached several times in chapel, and served as an unofficial chaplain to the seminary faculty. A visiting professor that year at Bethany was Dr. Hans-Werner Bartsch, of Frankfurt, Germany, one of the most distinguished New Testament scholars in Europe, and an outspoken pacifist. I took his course in Romans and found it a stimulating discipline. The Bartschs and we lived in adjoining apartments on campus and developed a deep friendship which has continued until now. Dr. Bartsch and Ilda had great empathy, for both were "brittle" diabetics. In later years I visited Bartschs in Lich, where they have a lovely home an hour from the Göethe Frei Universitat in Frankfurt, where he is professor of New Testament. He has contributed a number of excellent articles to *Brethren Life and Thought.*

I had a pleasant office at Bethany, and many good interviews with students. The basic idea of having a seasoned pastor share with students for several months is an excellent one. One thoughtful senior sat on my desk one day and said, "I haven't been sure of going into the ministry because I feared I would grow stale by middle age. You have showed me that such a fate isn't necessary! I'm going to be a pastor." He is today, and a good one.

It is encouraging to see that Bethany has strongly weathered the years when college rebels sometimes angrily rejected the ideals and goals of ministry, and were disruptive of seminary life. Today the seminary is stronger than ever, is attracting many excellent students, a large proportion of them women who show much promise.

I spent a week in the hospital during this period, and Ilda found the cold winds very dangerous to her health. So before winter came, after a delightful Thanksgiving family reunion with the Houffs and my father, Ilda and I took off for California in our heavily-laden Ford on Thanksgiving afternoon, November 25.

The drive to California was beautiful and restful. We had one especially joyous happening. On Saturday we stayed overnight in Albuquerque, New Mexico. Early Sunday morning we drove out to the Acoma Pueblo, some miles off our route. This is a very ancient village on a high, rugged mesa. We drove up the steep, rocky trail, and spent two or three hours looking, talking with the Indians, and taking pictures. I gave a noble-faced woman a dollar to let me take her picture as she took her fragrant loaves of fresh bread from a round adobe oven. She gave Ilda a big loaf of crusty bread. At noon, well on our way again, we ate half of the bread, spread thick with butter. As we ate it, remembering our delightful visit with the Indians, it seemed like a real communion!

Arriving in Bakersfield on the 29th, we were welcomed by the Marvin Belchers, and stayed with them five days until we found a comfortable little apartment very near our little church. This apartment was perfect for us, for Ilda was unable to do a great deal of housework. There was a swimming pool right by our door in the little apartment court.

Across the street was a fine estate with many trees, and a fascinating population of birds, most of them new to us.

The Bakersfield congregation was small, about one hundred fifty members, but loaded with talent and most responsive. Here for the first time, my salary was up to the denomination's pastors' salary scale! The church was quite overwhelmingly made up of educators. Among the fifty families, there were two school administrators, four principals, and at least twenty-two teachers, plus several retired school people! I was amazed, too, to find that we had many tall men! Our moderator, Wayne Carter, was six feet six inches tall. When we stood at the chancel steps to be installed, he stood above us with our district executive, and I have rarely felt so small.

The congregation responded warmly to my style of preaching and worship. There was an extraordinarily competent choir. The director, almost from the founding of the church, was Sherlo Shively, and his wife, Ila, was a talented and sensitive organist. The church sanctuary held about one hundred forty people and was acoustically excellent. So the music always sounded superb! In so small a congregation to have a balanced choir of eighteen persons, with many voices of solo quality, was like sharing with the celestial choir itself.

We soon were able to learn the names of everyone, and within a few months had visited all the homes of the congregation. We found a great variety of faith experiences in this small church. Several women had become deeply involved in a very popular but extremely fundamentalist Bible study fellowship which weekly attracted hundreds of women. The study materials and methods of the group were rigidly controlled and based on literalistic biblical interpretation. Even with this pervasive influence, the church was a united, warm and caring fellowship. Their solicitous love and concern for Ilda in her declining health soon developed very strong and caring relationships between pastor and people.

Soon after our arrival, our head usher, a genial and witty engineer, Don Mackenzie, told me, "The teachers run this church! I'd like to bring in enough engineers to swamp them!" The first three families we received into the church that year were of highway engineers! The church grew, not rapidly, but steadily, and the quality of church loyalty and the level of stewardship was very high. It was a wonderful place to have a more leisurely and less taxing ministry. The climate was good for us, and I was able to stay much closer to Ilda than in former years.

Before we went to California, many friends would say to us, "California? That's wonderful! Where in California?" When I would reply, "Bakersfield," the usual exclamation was, "Bakersfield! Why, I drove through there once, and it was hot as ----!" Bakersfield is the county seat of vast Kern County, at the south end of the Joaquin Valley. We found the city a beautiful place to live. Watered abundantly by the Kern River which tumbled through an immense rugged canyon from the snowy

Sierra Nevada, and by deep wells, the city of one hundred seventy-five thousand had beautiful trees, lawns and flowers everywhere. The city was surrounded by great irrigated ranches, growing cotton, fruits, vegetables, grapes, alfalfa, and an unbelievable variety of other farm products. On three sides were mountains. On the west, the coast ranges separated us from the Pacific Ocean. To the east were the southern ranges and plateaus of the Sierra Nevada, and joining them in a great tumbled arc of golden hills was the Tehachapi Range. Through much of the year the steep slopes of the lower ranges were a tawny golden color like a lion's skin. In March, if rains had been adequate, these hills quickly turned emerald green, tinted with thousands of acres of poppies, lupines, and owl clover. I soon became acquainted with the eloquent writings of John Muir and came to love the majestic mountains and limitless valleys of California as he did!

Don Mackenzie once said to me, "I've lived in Bakersfield twenty years; what I like about it is that in two hours I can be in the heart of Los Angeles, or in the snows of the High Sierras, or in the sand of the Mojave Desert, or on the beaches of the Pacific — and any of these is better than where I came from!"

Across the street from our little church was a beautiful large parochial school, belonging to St. Francis Catholic Church, which was a few blocks away. A few weeks after Christmas we attended a series of ecumenical services celebrating the Week of Prayer for Christian Unity, along with several members of our own church. Directly behind Ilda and me was a group of seven or eight Dominican sisters, teachers in St. Francis' school. The leader of the group, a vivacious and friendly woman, introduced herself as Sister Raphael, and then introduced the others. The sisters attended several of the week's meetings and invited us to a fireside conversation at their convent as part of the follow-up to the week of prayer. This friendly contact with the Catholic sisters was to have far-reaching consequences for me. At a later time, Sister Raphael invited me to visit and talk to her class in the school. She and Ilda became close friends, and when she began attending our Thursday evening Bible study group, she often stopped at our home for a cup of tea and good talk. When she was transferred back to her home city, Seattle, a year later, she wrote us occasionally and we greatly missed her friendship. Frequently she had attended our morning service, after directing a large choir of children at a mass in St. Francis Church. On one occasion, she invited six or eight leading clergymen and their wives to a gracious luncheon at the convent. The new spirit of Christian love so eloquently taught and nobly demonstrated by Pope John XXIII had apparently caught on with this group of dedicated Dominican teachers. Their school was an excellent one, and the neighborhood loved them!

District activities in the Pacific Southwest Conference and ecumenical activities locally attracted me, but were never again so heavy as they had been in Virginia. I served one more year on the General Brotherhood

Board, as chairman of the Foreign Missions Commission, and was chairman for two or three years of our Interchurch Relations Committee. The latter took considerable time and energy, as we were engaged in long and serious discussions with the American Baptists and two or three smaller church bodies, exploring cooperation in depth and possibilities of merger.

It may be well to digress here a bit to catch up on my involvement in Brethren ecumenism. When the Consultation on Church Union (COCU) began in 1962, sparked by the (Eugene Carson) Blake-Bishop Pike proposals, the Church of the Brethren was invited to send an observer to the annual meetings of the group. By 1965, we were invited to become full partners in the Consultation. The General Board and Annual Conference gave this matter serious consideration, and asked the Fraternal Relations Committee to bring a recommendation to the 1966 Conference in Louisville, Kentucky. There was great interest in the matter, and our committee gave it intensive and prayerful study. We recommended that we stay open to further light, to continue full and responsible involvement in the Councils of Churches, to seek close relationships with church bodies similar to our own in faith and polity, but not to accept full membership in the Consultation on Church Union. The leadership of the church was seriously divided on the issue. My brother Jesse was the chief protagonist for COCU membership, and I took an opposite view. For a time our own private fraternal relationship was strained. The nearly full day's debate at Annual Conference was spirited, intelligent, and high-minded. The vote of Conference to accept the committee report was overwhelming — perhaps six to one.

While the outcome was a bitter disappointment to the dedicated Brethren thinkers and leaders who saw a bright hope in COCU, subsequent developments have, I believe, proved the rightness of the conference's decision. The real thrust of ecumenism since then has not been in the direction of giant mergers which would result in a monolithic church with a ponderous beaurocracy, but in many trusting areas of cooperation in local communities and in shared program with denominations which have a common heritage and faith. The Brethren are now in many fruitful projects where two or more local churches of different denominations have successfully united. There have been good experiences where Brethren have joined with American Baptists, Disciples, or congregations of the United Church of Christ.

In the Pacific Southwest Conference, I served three years on the District Board and one year as moderator. On the local level, I served three years as president of the Greater Bakersfield Council of Churches, and on the Board of Directors of the Church of the Sequoias.

One of the excellent Mennonite-sponsored community Mental Health Centers, Kern View, was in Bakersfield. About 1968, a new director, Larry Yoder, took over the administration of the center. He and his wife became active members of our church, holding dual membership with their home church, Goshen Mennonite, in Indiana. One of Larry's moves to strengthen Kern View was to have several non-Mennonite directors on his board. I was elected to the board, and served two years as its vice chairman. For a number of reasons, Kern View had not had good relationships with the medical community. There has been a long up-hill struggle, but now it has an honored place and is doing great service in the area. I was proud to be connected with Kern View, and to work with Yoder.

The later years of my pastoral ministry seemed to bring an ever-increasing load of counselling work. At Bakersfield I was deeply involved in personal and family counselling. One person suffering deep depression and suicidal tendencies seemed to need an enormous amount of time. Ultimately she recovered fully and became a radiant and active member of the church, but in outgrowing her need of counselling, seemed to reject me as minister and turned away from a good relationship, to my deep sorrow. In the years of my ministry there, this and a devastating failure in my attempt to hold a breaking family together, brought me deep disappointment. I had not had adequate training for counselling, and it was salutary for me to realize I could not win every time! I rejoice in what success I have had in bringing persons in all my pastorates closer to God, seeing hundreds commit themselves to faithful Christian discipleship, a score of young persons sharing my vision of ministry and committing themselves to it. Yet my failures make me feel very humble, and I grieve that I could not do more for persons who depended so greatly on my help in finding wholeness and a new life!

Not only in my professional life as a minister, but also in the life of our family we have experienced both light and shadow, great joys and heavy disappointments. I had cherished the hope that one or both of my sons would follow me into the professional ministry. Both of them have found their life work instead in teaching. I rejoice in their commitment to this area of ministry — Robert as a college professor, Donald as a visual literacy specialist.

In August, 1967, Donald was married to Virginia Flory. This marriage ended in divorce after she completed her medical training. He married Beverly Brown of Richmond, Virginia, on December 20, 1975. They have a strong and happy marriage and have a lovely home in Richmond.

Ruth Ann and Warren experienced deep tragedy. Their first child, an angelic little girl named Daren, was born in April, 1968. Two weeks before her third birthday she died of cancer. They had another daughter, Megan, born in December, 1971, who is a tall and sensitive third-grader now. They live near Hartford, Connecticut, where Warren is a teacher, and Ruth Ann is active in community affairs.

Robert received his Ph. D. at the University of Wisconsin in 1966, and since then has been on the faculty of Elizabethtown College. Their four children are grown. Our family was saddened by the ending of their marriage also in divorce, after twenty-eight years of marriage. I have sometimes taken undue pride in saying that if couples follow the counsel a pastor gives in adequate premarital counselling, and maintain a genuinely Christian family life, the marriage will never fail. But while I believe my sons and their companions really tried, their marriages did fail at last. We have learned to hold each other in abiding love even through all of these darker valleys of our lives and have come through with stronger ties than ever. We believe that for the mistakes and wrong turns that lead to the death of a marriage there is a divine forgiveness and grace to rebuild a life, with new and even better relationships.

When a loved family member dies, as with little Daren, we have learned to accept these partings with courage, and faith, and invincible hope. All these dark valleys are not life's last word—there is hope and renewal, healing and renewal. This my family and I surely know.

We greatly enjoyed our life in Bakersfield. It was easy to find the kinds of fruits Ilda needed, and we soon found for her a good medical doctor who was very understanding of her needs. The vacation trips to mountain or desert or seashore were invigorating. Also she was happy to be rather near to her brother Desmond, who lived just three hours away, in Orange.

In 1968 we planned a great adventure. I recruited a congenial group of twelve persons for a tour of Bible lands and Europe in the early summer. In April, Ilda flew east to be with Ruth Ann when Daren was born. She stayed there several weeks and also visited other family members until our tour party started eastward. I joined her in Connecticut, then we all gathered at Kennedy Airport for our great trip. The tour was a marvelous experience. I had for many years hoped to see the Holy Land and have the scenes of Bible history come alive. In Israel, we had an unusually well-informed and articulate guide. He was a Rumanian Jew, a survivor of three years in Hitler's concentration camps. He was a devout Bible scholar, at home in many languages. We were most fortunate to have his gentle, inspiring guidance. He had been James Michener's guide during the months of his research at Megiddo, for *The Source*.

In Jerusalem, we stayed several nights at the American Colony Inn and met the gracious ninety-one-year-old Bertha Spafford Vester, who was part of the original American Colony there and founder of the famed Children's Hospital on the old city wall. It would require a whole book to describe the rich experiences of this tour of Bible lands. It was for all of us a tremendous spiritual experience, to know that we were actually walking in the footsteps of Jesus and Paul, Abraham and David and Jeremiah, sailing on the startling blue loveliness of the Sea of Galilee. But this is not a travelogue. Suffice it to say that for Ilda and me, it was both fulfillment and promise. God willing, we would come back and spend time in more study and reflection. For her it was not to be.

Just a few incidents of human interest can be told here. While we had excellent accommodations everywhere on the tour, in Haifa we stayed a night in the magnificent Dan Carmel Hotel, thirteen hundred feet above the spectacular Bay of Acre on Mount Carmel. Here the four couples of our party were lodged in four luxurious penthouse suites! The only reason I could think of was that with a name like mine, the management must have concluded that I was the rabbi of some wealthy California temple with vast riches to pour into Israel's development! We never did disillusion them! My exuberant old colleague, Wilbur Liskey, when shown into his suite, went about exclaiming over and over, "Wow! Wow!"

Our guide, Willy, (he wouldn't use his last name) was not only extremely helpful; he liked our party! He told me that many parties who go with him are biblical literalists, who mistrust his biblical expertise and try to convert him; or they are wealthy Jews from Miami or New York whose only questions are, "Was this built with American dollars? How much did it cost?" I think he appreciated our reverent openness, our keen interest in the Israel of today as well as the sacred past!

Our tour included three of the sites of the "Seven Churches of Asia," Smyrna, Ephesus and Pergamum, Athens and Corinth, Rome, Geneva and London. We arrived back in New York just in time to get to Ocean Grove, New Jersey, for the opening of the 1968 Annual Conference.

No thoughtful person could live and serve in Christian ministry during the 1960s without being deeply troubled and moved by the vast and profound turmoil of that devastating decade. The civil rights movement, the obscene horror of the Vietnam War, the assassinations of President John F. Kennedy, Dr. Martin Luther King, Jr. and Robert Kennedy almost made one despair for the future of our beloved America. While we lived at Oakton, I gladly and resolutely participated in the great "March for Justice," and heard King's superb Christian oration, "I Have a Dream." I was deeply committed to a Christian witness for racial justice and integration, though my stand met serious opposition in the churches I served. Even at Bakersfield, when I joined in the forefront of a great demonstration the Sunday after King's murder and raised my voice publicly for justice for blacks and farm laborers, there was sharp dissension in the church. I am sure that those who questioned what I thought was a prophetic stand for justice, were also committed to Christian righteousness. But Kern County was conservative, and had an unsavory record of rigid opposition to Caesar Chavez's Farm Labor Union, and of indifference to the plight of minorities. There were instances of police brutality in Bakersfield and it was hard for our Brethren to take a strong stand against the tide of conservatism. John Steinway's *Grapes of Wrath* was banned from Kern County libraries and schools and the support of the churches for Chavez and the farm workers was unpopular in the community.

I never felt called to go to Selma and march with the blacks, or to join the Farm Workers' picket lines in the fields and vineyards in California. Perhaps had I been twenty years younger, I would have done so. But I tried to be always on the side of the poor, the downtrodden, the oppressed, in my preaching and writing. I earnestly tried to be a reconciler. I have deeply admired the courageous witness of King and Chavez, both uncompromising Christian leaders; and of persons like Ralph Smeltzer in our own church, whose quiet reconciling ministry across a whole generation helped greatly in the quest for justice and peace.

My understanding of the Gospel during all the years of my ministry, and especially through these difficult times, has been that there can be no dichotomy between a personal and social Gospel. There is one Gospel — the Good News of God through Christ for the salvation of the whole person — both as an individual and the family and society of which he is a part.

My work with the Inter-Church Relations Committee of the Church of the Brethren was challenging and rewarding. During these later years of my involvement, I twice attended the annual American Baptist Convention. The ecumenical officer of the Baptists, Dr. Robert G. Torbet, became a close friend. He and I worked together, especially in the preparation of a booklet which was designed to help Baptists and Brethren to learn to know each other. In 1968, Ilda and I attended the Baptist convention in Boston, just before leaving for Israel. I was asked to bring Brethren greetings in a big evening assembly, in which Bishop Fulton J. Sheen was the preacher. His sermon could well have been preached by a Brethren! In 1969, I attended the convention in Seattle and gave a brief prepared address, in the form of a dialogue with a Baptist leader. During these years we worked out a pattern of cooperative work with the Baptists which has proved very beneficial. But we both shied away from complete merger. Brethren saw too much congregational autonomy and fundamentalism among Baptists, and Baptists were shy of our total rejection of war and thought we might be too centralized in polity.

In our Pacific Coast Conference (district) there was great need for strong leadership, and I served on the Conference Board. The 1969 convocation, when I was moderator, was for the first time held in Bakersfield. The excellent facilities of the First Congregational Church proved ideal for our meetings. Eastern Brethren are amazed at the distances travelled for western district functions. Bakersfield was central; people came five hundred to six hundred miles from the Arizona Churches, and as much as four hundred miles from the churches in northern California.

The Ecumenical Institute of Chicago gained a strong foothold in Southern California, and several Brethren pastors and churches were drawn into its orbit. The off-beat, almost heretical theology of the Institute, and the rigid structure and methodology they promoted, proved a kiss of death to the churches. So far as I know, not one pastor involved in the Institute continued long in the ministry, and they succeeded in dividing, confusing, and alienating their congregations. Ten years after this disruptive influence, several of the churches in the Los Angeles area are still suffering from the dissension and confusion of that period. California has been noted for exotic native forms of religion, but this was an import!

The year 1969 was a busy one for me, and it was an anxious year. Ilda's health continued to worsen, and she was hospitalized every two or three months for severe complications of her diabetic condition and weakening heart. By early 1970, we felt that I should retire from active ministry. We decided to move to Sebring, Florida. In early February, I flew to Florida and purchased a mobile home in a park where many of the residents were old friends. A few days after my return home, Ilda's heart condition worsened, and severe uremic poisoning made it impossible for her to remain at home. She entered the hospital and had the best of medical and nursing care. Our church people were most solicitous for us, and helpful. On the morning of March 3, 1970, when I came to her room, I found she had had a massive cerebral accident. I stayed close to her throughout the day. Late at night she seemed to be resting more quietly. I planned to go home for a few hours of sleep. I kissed her, and said some words we often used, "Goodnight darling; I'll see you in the morning." She smiled as if she had heard. I had been at home only an hour when the head nurse called me to say that she had died! A long and very richly rewarding chapter of my life was over. I spent the next several hours alone in our apartment, weeping, remembering, turning to the great comforting words of the Bible, and listening to the superb music of Brahms' *Requiem,* which we both had loved. Then I called our children and other family people in the east. Before dawn, I wrote a letter, which I sent to our church people and many friends. Here it is:

March 4, 1970

My Dear Friends:

I am writing this in the early morning hours. Just before midnight, my beloved wife Ilda slipped quietly out of this life into the glorious wonderland of the presence of God.

All day yesterday after a stroke which came in the early morning, she slept, but tossed in fever and some inner distress.

During the evening she was resting more quietly. When I left her a few hours ago to come home for a little sleep, I kissed her and said some words which have long had special meaning for us, "Goodnight, darling; I'll see you in the morning!"

Well, now she knows the dawning of a far more wonderful morning than ever before.

Many of us have hoped and prayed for a miracle of healing. When she was first afflicted by diabetes, our good doctors told me that with care she might live ten years. That was thirty-six years ago! We have reared our family and shared a very rich and rewarding life ministry for nearly forty-seven years.

And the greatest miracle of all has come — the miracle of the resurrection for her. For we have long believed that it is God's will that she be well and strong and whole. Now it is His will that her healing come only through the resurrection; thanks be to God for this!

You have known Ilda for a few years. Think how I have been blessed, having her as my wife, my partner in the ministry, my comrade of the road for all these wonderful years.

I have often tried to comfort others in the sorrow of bereavement. Now I know that the faith I have commended to you is sound and that in the Valley of the Shadow of Death there is indeed nothing to fear.

I feel very much alone this morning; yet it's a loneliness filled with a sense of Ilda's nearness. The things she used and cared for, the beautiful things she has made, pictures she has painted, are all around me. And the strong, tender comforting presence of God is very near and real to me.

We shall have a service of memory for Ilda at our church on Sunday afternoon. Her tired body will be laid to rest in the beautiful quiet cemetery on the hillside above her home church in West Virginia near her father, two brothers and her sister. Just across the valley is the old home where she grew up and where we were married.

So many of you have brought comfort and help to us in these long months of Ilda's illness and suffering. She wants me to say thank you, and that she has greatly loved you and been blessed by you.

Let us thank God together for the quiet grace, the warmth, the compassion, the gay and joyful courage which were so much of Ilda's style of living.

Please keep me in your prayers,

Yours in hope and love of God,
Edward K. Ziegler

Bob immediately flew out to be with me, and then Desmond and Irene Bittinger came, too. We planned a memorial service in the Bakersfield Church which was a great, moving, triumphant worship experience. My close friend, Dr. Tom Toler, pastor of First Christian Church, presided. Truman Northup, our conference executive, preached, and Monsignor Leddy, pastor of St. Francis' Church, led prayers. Our choir sang the magnificent setting of "For All the Saints," and "Abide with Me, 'Tis Eventide."

Ilda's body was flown back to Oakland, Maryland. I flew the next day, and another service was held in her home church at Eglon. Here all the rest of the family came, and hundreds of friends from the churches we had served in Virginia also. Wayne Zunkel, Bob's pastor, gave a profoundly helpful meditation, and at last Ilda's worn body was laid to rest in the family plot in the quiet beauty of the West Virginia hills.

When I returned home, the church people urged me not to retire then, but to stay on where we had had such a good experience in the past four years. It was the right thing to do! The man who sold me the mobile home in Florida gladly returned my down payment, and I returned to my ministry—lonely, but with a rich treasure of memories and the gracious and caring fellowship of a great little church to minister God's consolations to me as I continued to minister to them.

CHAPTER 10

Retired — End or Beginning?

Ilda's death early in 1970 changed my life in many ways. After I returned from the memorial services at Eglon, and visits with my family, I tried to pick up the pieces of my life. The people of the church and many others in the community were kind, hospitable, and understanding. When I preached my Easter sermon a few weeks later, my subject was "My Personal Easter Faith." I began by saying, "Never before has the resurrection been so real to me, so comforting and inspiring. For I have had my Good Friday, and Easter has dawned with greater assurance and splendor than ever before. I know Jesus lives, and because He lives, Ilda lives, and I too shall live!"

I planned now, after counselling with Truman Northup and our local church leaders, to continue my pastorate until the end of the pastoral year in 1971. Since this was near the time of the fiftieth anniversary of my ordination, the church kept me on as an associate until December first of that year, even though my able successor, J. Calvin Keeling, came on September first.

My marriage with Ilda had been so good, so completely fulfilling, that I felt that I did not want to stay unmarried very long. Before her death, Ilda had urged me to find some gracious woman who could be my companion. Among the many letters of condolence and support I received was one from Mary Vivolo, the former Sister Raphael. She had left the Dominican order because she felt she could no longer be comfortable in the structured life of the order. She was now teaching in Mountlake Christian School near Seattle. Her letter was so gracious and helpful that I soon began corresponding rather regularly. Later I visited her in Seattle, and in long conversations, we believed it to be God's will for us to marry.

That summer she moved back to Bakersfield and began teaching in junior high school. As I shared our plans with my children and brother and sisters, I found them all warmly supportive. Before Mary left Seattle, I met her aged mother. It was quite a shock for her to realize that her youngest daughter, who had been in the order for twenty years, had not only left the order, but was about to marry an elderly Protestant clergyman! But she was most gracious about it. When I told her about myself and my love for Mary, she said in her accented English as she laid her hand on mine, "Mary is grown up. She has made this choice. All I can say is God bless her, and God bless you, too!" Mother Vivolo was past eighty then, a stately, beautiful person. I did not meet many of Mary's family at that time. When the next July her older sister Lucy died, we went to the funeral and I met all of them. Mary was the youngest of ten children. Her parents had emigrated from a little town high in the mountains of southern Italy, about 1910. Mary was brought up in an ethnic parish of the Roman Church in Seattle and had a good relationship with her parents. Now the family ties are quite weak since the deaths of Lucy and their mother. Mary keeps in close touch with two of her sisters and one of her nieces.

We planned to be married after Christmas. But in October I became critically ill. After I returned from the hospital, family and friends thought we should marry sooner, so that I need not remain alone longer. We were married in our church on November 25; Paul E. Miller, a long time colleague and friend of mine officiated, and Truman Northup was my best man. None of my family could be present. Desmond and Irene Bittinger came, but because of rain and heavy traffic, arrived an hour after the wedding! I do not understand why, but a complete drought for two hundred days was broken that evening by an inch of rain!

We travelled east for our Christmas vacation and visited my children. All of them welcomed Mary most warmly. A part of our visit was an anxious time, for Ruth Ann's little Daren was very ill with a rare cancer which was almost always terminal. Daren died in March of 1971. I was with them when she died, and Mary flew back also for the memorial service. Warren and Ruth Ann were surrounded by many friends and had good pastoral care through the months of Daren's illness. They were courageous and calm, but their grief was very deep. God found the most perfect way to assuage their sorrow, giving them another beautiful baby girl on December 28, whom they named Megan.

In June, we went to Annual Conference at St. Petersburg, Florida. Mary had become strongly attached to the Church of the Brethren. Shortly before we were married she united with the church; at Easter time she requested baptism and it was my joy to administer baptism by immersion to her. But the vast hubbub of Annual Conference was overwhelming for her. She is a shy person, and everyone seemed to know me. I introduced her to many hundreds of people. It was too much to absorb at once, and she hasn't greatly cared for the conferences since then. She was somewhat disconcerted also by the demonstrations and confrontations that at that time seemed to be the style of Conference participation of some younger people. I shared her dismay at this!

A few days after Conference, while visiting my family, we received news of her sister Lucy's death, and flew to Seattle for the funeral. A few months later, her mother also died. Thus my chief contacts with her family were in these times of grief and mourning.

I completed my term as pastor at the end of August 1971. We had bought a beautiful little home on the eastern part of Bakersfield and found it a great joy. I planted many roses, and fixed up a very comfortable study. Mary was now transferred to a new elementary school not far from our new home. We hoped we could spend many good years there. I was teaching a Bible class made up of older women of many denominations, and settled down to plan some writing and what I thought would be a fairly leisurely retirement!

Our church people planned a sparkling celebration for the fiftieth anniversary of my ordination. Sherlo and Ila Shively did much of the planning. The big event was a fantastic dinner party at First Congregational Church. My son Bob flew out, some two hundred friends and colleagues were there, and it was a deeply moving evening. Vernard Eller, Tom Toler, and Truman Northup all said some things which touched and almost embarrassed me.

The Shivelys had written many people across the country, and the responses of letters filled a big scrapbook which is now one of my most cherished treasures. The church also gave me a fine watch, which continues to mark the golden hours of my crowded retirement years.

I had served three years on the board of the Church of the Sequoias. This was an inter-denominational project designed to provide religious services in Sequoia and Kings Canyon National Parks. I was appointed resident minister for the organization for 1972. The plan for this project was to invite ministers to come up to the park early in a given week, spend a few days vacation, be available for counselling campers, and then conduct a Sunday service of worship. The Church of the Sequoias had cabins or tents at several locations which were provided free for the guest ministers. In addition, each year ten or twelve seminary and college students were employed in the park concessions, who assisted or supplemented the work of the guest minister.

As resident minister, my task was to recruit the guest ministers, arrange the schedule of services, see that living quarters and equipment were all in order, prepare liturgies and have an adequate supply of bulletins for the services, supervise the religious activities of the students who were recruited and trained for summer service by the Christian Ministry in the National Parks staff, serve as counselor and chaplain for the students, and be the liaison person with the National Park Service and the concession company which ran all the lodgings, camp grounds and stores. Each week, I collated the records of our work and banked the funds received in the offerings.

I received a modest salary, and from early June to Labor Day, Mary and I lived in a small and somewhat decrepit and weatherbeaten trailer (eight by thirty-two feet) in a grove of ancient Sequoias near Giant Forest. The months from February to June were busy with correspondence and planning. As soon as the snow cover permitted in May, with a number of volunteers, we got things out of storage and prepared the cabins and tents for use. On a hilltop just above our trailer was a group of cabins, some for summer park ranger naturalists, some for guest ministers of the Church of the Sequoias; so we were never lonely!

Sunday services were held in the outdoor amphitheaters which were used nightly by the naturalist rangers for their informative lectures and picture shows. In three of the locations outside the Park but in the National Forest, the Church of the Sequoias had its own outdoor meeting places. Our Sunday services began on Sunday of the Memorial Day weekend—where there was no snow—and continued until Labor Day weekend. In one or two of the less frequented areas, our attendances were quite small. But at others there were hundreds of worshipers and great moments of high inspiration. I note in my log book that at a service in a forest campground one Sunday there were three present, including the guest minister! But at Grant Grove, attendance ranged well over two hundred Sunday after Sunday!

We had eleven students recruited by the Christian Ministry in National Parks staff. They were a varied and delightful group! A black Anglican priest from Nigeria on a World Council of Churches scholarship; a track star from a southern college who climbed every Sierra peak within miles in his spare time; a Harvard Divinity student, who claimed to be an evangelical Unitarian; a Nazarene girl, who did a superb job teaching children each Sunday morning and worked as a cafeteria waitress; a young Lutheran teacher, who preached great sermons and went on to be an educational missionary in New Guinea—these were some of our group!

Our summer was full and happy. We had many picnic dinners with groups of guest ministers and with groups of students. Every week or two we returned to our home in Bakersfield for supplies for ourselves and for the program and the guest quarters. By the end of the summer, we had had over a hundred services, with total attendance well over eight thousand. There were many expressions of appreciation from tourists who found that to share in a beautiful worship surrounded by the timeless grandeur of the granite mountains and the trees which were tall and old when Jesus lived in Galilee, gave a glorious new dimension to their vacation. Though I did conduct a few services myself, Mary and I usually worshipped at one of the campgrounds. I especially recall a service at Silver City, high in the Sierras, conducted by a Lutheran pastor from a university center. A woman who ran the resort nearby led the singing with guitar and a beautiful voice. In another great service at Grant Grove, a Methodist pastor from a church in Long Beach preached a most appropriate sermon, and then he and the black Nigerian priest served communion to over two hundred worshippers. At the same time the Nazarene student with some volunteer help taught some sixty children under the trees nearby.

There were many delightful incidents in this busy summer. Black bears made their rounds nearly every night to collect goodies from our garbage. One bear learned to break into the ground floor pantry at the Giant Forest restaurant, and ate cases of Jello pudding! Another snatched a whole roasted chicken from a guest minister's table. Perhaps the same beggar pried open a minister's car trunk and made off with a week's supply of meat while the family slept in a tent ten feet away!

Late one evening Mary baked chocolate chip cookies. About midnight our friendly bear caught the tantalizing aroma and tried to pry off our trailer door. Finally in frustration he stood up and beat on the wall in rage, then wandered away! Many of the guest ministers had a great supply of bear stories to take home with them!

An unexpected diversion was the three of four couples who wanted to be married in the park. So I had weddings on Sunset Rock, where the couple and guests could look out over a hundred miles of mountain grandeur during the ceremony. One couple wanted to be married on top of Mount Whitney, but the park superintendent turned that one down!

One event was a great satisfaction to us. A group of thirty-two young Japanese bankers came to the United States for a summer of special training. The inter-cultural organization which arranged their trip asked Bakersfield Kiwanis Clubs to host them for a few days of orientation. As chairman of the International Relations Committee for the Kiwanis district, I worked on plans. We had them tour Kings Canyon and Sequoia on their first day, and we were hosts at our trailer for a picnic supper of Mary's gorgeous hamburgers, Kentucky Fried Chicken, and melons. With a few fellow Kiwanians, a Japanese teacher, and a German exchange student, there were forty of us.

The Japanese were most cordial, appreciative and polite. Our neighborhood clean-up bear really had a sumptuous feast that night. He ate all scraps, all chicken bones and melon rinds, then finally staggered down the hill to sleep it off!

Though this was an unusually hot and dry summer in the mountains, I found one hundred twenty-five kinds of wild flowers, and many birds, besides seeing many squirrels, bears and a bobcat. I caught two small trout; there were more anglers than trout that summer! One evening in late summer, I showed slides of wild flowers of the park to a gathering of the park naturalists.

It had been my hope that I could serve at least two years as resident minister, but that summer I received an invitation to come to India to spend a year as a visiting professor at the Gujarat United School of Theology in Ahmedabad, which I had helped to establish many years earlier. The offer seemed very attractive. After much deliberation we decided to go to India the next year, and after that settle in the east somewhere to be nearer to my family and to have more opportunity for the kinds of teaching/preaching occasional work I hoped to do. In preparation, we sold our home and most of our furniture. We planned to go east and store our goods at my sister's home in Maryland, and to stay with her until our visas would permit us to go to India.

In mid-September, we had an eventful trip to Yellowstone National Park for the Annual Meeting of the Christian Ministry in the National Parks, which coincided with the Centennial celebration of the National Park Service. The three day celebration was a movable feast, with meetings at Mammoth Hot Springs, Old Faithful, and Jackson's Lake, in the Grand Teton Park. The conference and the three thousand mile trip were a memorable climax to our adventurous summer in the mountains.

On our return we shipped our library and the few furnishings and goods we wanted to keep, and late in September started a leisurely four thousand mile trip to Maryland, by way of Seattle, the Rockies and Black Hills and finally to the Eastern Shore of Maryland.

As things worked out, we were not to get to India at all. Relations between India and the United States were strained, and we could not get visas. So after two months of frustrating waiting, we began to explore for a permanent home in the east. An old colleague, Merlin Garber, urged us to settle in Frederick, Maryland. He offered me an attractive position on the staff of the Frederick Church, now the largest Church of the Brethren. I was to share in preaching, direct a lay academy, teach, and head up the Key '73 evangelistic effort. It would be a faith venture, he said, but the church would provide housing allowance or some such help. He helped us to find a comfortable apartment near the church and introduced Mary to the personnel director of the public school system of the county. We had explored quite widely, and this seemed to us the best place to settle and build our lives into a strong Christian community, since the hope of going to India had faded. So on December 1, 1972, we moved to Frederick. Mary soon had a good full-time teaching position in Liberty Elementary School, some ten miles from home. She was amazed at the generous salary offer she had from the county, and began a teaching career which has been very rewarding, though demanding. She is still at the same school as I write today!

I shared in the ministry of the Frederick Church for nearly nine months, preaching about three times a month, teaching a fine group of thirty adults in the church's Lay Academy, and writing a series of Bible Study materials which were used by six churches. Each Monday morning, Dr. Garber, John David Bowman, the young associate pastor, and I spent an hour or two in Bible study for the next Sunday's preaching, and in prayer. In many ways it was a good experience. The Frederick Church had grown rapidly during the ten years of Garber's ministry, but was not deeply involved in outreach, nor had there been a strong program to prepare the hundreds of new members for active discipleship. I do not regret these months of ministry, for I believe sharing the Gospel with integrity and zeal in teaching and preaching is its own reward. I can also say that there seemed to be real appreciation for my work among many of the Frederick people.

A promising facet of the church's program was the beginning of a satellite program at Walkersville, seven miles north. Here the Maryland Baptist Association had acquired land and planned to build a college. The only building actually built was a large chapel. When the venture failed, the land was sold to a developer. After two or three years, the Frederick Church bought the chapel and started holding services. As hundreds of new homes were built in the mushrooming community around the chapel, this promised to be a vital growing edge for the congregation.

In 1974, the substantial group of members in the area petitioned District Conference for fellowship status, which was granted. The Frederick Church undertook to complete payment for the property, and the new congregation began carrying its own program, with John David Bowman as pastor. The new group was creative and progressive, and there is every prospect that this will become a strong congregation.

The summer of 1973 was a time of great adventure for us. We spent six weeks in Europe, on an itinerary we planned ourselves, travelling several thousand miles by train and absorbing the beauty of the land and the rich historical and cultural heritage we so deeply cherish. Luxembourg, Paris, London, Amsterdam, Vienna, Innsbruck, Geneva, Naples, Florence, Munich—these were all filled with adventure for us. As we look back on our grand tour there were several highlights: an all-day steamer trip going up the Rhine River from Cologne to Frankfurt; a leisurely overnight visit to Schwarzenau, the cradle of our Brethren faith; then two wonderful days with Ruth and Hans-Werner Bartsch, in their lovely home in Lich. While Hans-Werner made a necessary trip to Frankfurt, Ruth drove us high into the Vogelberg mountains. There I stood in the walled, now dry spring which was the site of St. Boniface's first baptism in Germany. We found Dr. Bartsch almost in despair about the present weakness of the German church and deeply indignant about our country's tragic and terribly immoral Vietnam war. His views, we found, are paralleled by most thoughtful Christian leaders in Europe.

Another high adventure was our excursion out from Naples by train and bus to Accerno, a lovely little town high in the Appenine Mountains, the home of Mary's parents. No one spoke or understood English. But a young priest was very helpful. Mary's small Italian vocabulary and the friendly villagers, made the day a happy experience. The priest found for us a beautiful white-haired lady who proved to be Mary's cousin! We attended a lovely guitar mass in the village church where Mary's father, Raffaello Vivolo, had served as an altar boy, and where he and Giovannina Cappetto were married nearly seventy years earlier!

We attended church each of the five Sundays we were in Europe—the American Church in Paris, where an old friend, Baptist Ed Tuller, was pastor; a large Reformed Church in Amsterdam, where we shared in a communion service, and sang old Dutch Reformed hymns; mass in German in a beautiful baroque Dominican Church in Vienna; a disappointing English service on a rainy Sunday in Geneva; and then the sprightly guitar mass in Accerno. I am sure the Dutch sermon was scholarly, though I couldn't understand much. The sermon in Vienna, in German was excellent; and Mary said the sermon in Italian, in Accerno, also was very good!

We spent nine days in Switzerland without seeing the Alps! It was cloudy and rainy most of the time. For sheer beauty, we loved Innsbruck, the serene Eder Valley around Schwarzenau, and the old city of Lucerne on what must be one of the loveliest lakes in all Europe.

From October 1973 to June 1974, I served as interim pastor at Manassas, Virginia, commuting two or three days a week, and both of us spending Sunday there. The stimulating summer I spent there in 1927 was still a fragrant memory. Now to return to a strong, progressive church no longer rural, was a fine interlude! Our district executive, Donald Rowe, believes that most congregations ought to have an interim pastor while making a thorough study of needs and a careful search for a new permanent pastor. My experience at Manassas, and in 1976, at Westminster, Maryland, strongly confirms this view; not only did I find it a good opportunity for ministry, I found that the congregations were united and strengthened by my months of work. I think I did some of the best preaching I have ever done in those interim ministries. Then when John Bowman rather suddenly resigned from our Glade Valley Church, I served eight months there also as interim minister. Because this congregation is small, and only trying its wings, I served practically full-time, especially in the first several months of my term.

Because of Mary's teaching position, we do not want to move away, and at seventy-five, I am finding many other interesting and demanding things to do! However, I did serve the Flower Hill Church, in the suburbs of Washington, for four months in late 1978. The deep interest in our heritage sparked by the American Bicentennial, and the cultural splash aroused by *Roots*, led me to study the lives of nineteenth century Brethren leaders. Out of my study, I have prepared a series of monologues, impersonating the famous Brethren martyr, Elder John Kline of Virginia; the intinerant preacher/theologian, Peter Nead; and the scholarly founder of *Messenger*, Henry Kurtz. Thus far I have given the John Kline program—in appropriate costume—in many churches, several camps, and a college convocation. It seems to be a novel and effective way to make our rich heritage come alive.

Over Christmas in 1974, I led a tour party of seventeen persons to Israel and Greece. Again, this proved to be a profound spiritual pilgrimage. Highlights were: Christmas eve in the Shepherd's Fields and Bethlehem; a lovely Christmas day at Jericho, Masada and Qumran; and a beautiful Upper Room communion service for our party in Kibbutz Nof Ginnosar, overlooking the sea of Galilee.

As the story of my pilgrimage up to this time draws to a close, a few words about my family may be in order. Robert and Connie spent his sabbatical year of 1976-77 in Australia, as a visiting professor. Mary and I had a wonderful vacation in 1977, visiting them and other friends in Australia, and in several of the South Pacific Islands. Their sons are in the west, their daughters married and living near Elizabethtown. Robert has returned to Australia, teaching and organizing a graduate department in Churchlands Teachers' College in Perth.

Donald and Beverly have a lovely home and creative careers in Richmond, Virginia. Ruth Ann and her husband Warren live near Hartford, Connecticut, where Warren teaches and Ruth Ann is deeply involved in community affairs. Their daughter Megan is a tall, shy, lovely third-grader.

Mary and I moved out into the lovely rolling countryside of Frederick County on December 1, 1973. Here we lived more than five years in a big comfortable old farm house. From my study window in the converted summer kitchen, I could look across alfalfa fields and fence rows to the quiet somber loveliness of the Catoctin Mountains, six miles away. Occasionally deer or foxes crossed the fields near the house. We grew hundreds of tulips and had a good garden. We also had a big, friendly, lazy, but shy Bassett hound, named Morris Conrad Junior. At this writing time, we live in a spacious and comfortable apartment in Frederick, quite close to the mountains.

We have a good marriage. It is a fine sharing partnership. I have learned to cook, and enjoy preparing a nourishing dinner as much as I do writing a chapter or preparing a sermon. Mary cares deeply about my health and welfare, is quite protective, and concerned that I do not undertake tasks beyond my strength. She is an excellent teacher, very professional and conscientious. Rather reluctantly, she has carried a heavy load of responsibilities in Christian nurture in our church. We have shared our life now for nine years, and look to the future with radiant joy and hope!

CHAPTER 11

Putting It On Paper

For the past forty years, I have considered writing a vital part of my ministry. Even earlier, during our India years, the *Gospel Messenger* used many of my news articles, and many pictures which I had taken. I also wrote occasionally for the *Indian Witness,* a Methodist publication, and the *National Christian Council Review* of India. I noted earlier the beginnings of the little newspaper *Ajavaliu,* and the surprising fate of my first book, *A Book of Worship for Village Churches.*

Most of the books I have written, especially in the earlier years, are about worship. Agricultural Missions, Inc. published several of them. One book, *Rural Preaching,* was published by a commercial publishing company. Later publications have been of a wider variety of subjects. Of course most of the earlier works are now out of print.

In addition, I have written chapters for other books: *Watchers of the Springs* (a book of rural sermons), published by the Virginia Council of Churches. *Voices of the Ecumenical Movement*—a Festschrift honoring W. A. Visser t' Hooft (German). *The Church of the Brethren Past and Present* (in German and English), and a bicentennial volume published by Maryland Churches United, entitled *Christian Bicentennial Witness.*

Quite a bit of my writing has been for periodicals such as *Messenger;* and the *Brethren Leader* and the *Brethren Teachers' Monthly,* both no longer published. It has been a particular satisfaction to write devotional materials for Brethren publications and for the National Council of Churches, and several series of lessons for the *Teachers Monthly* and its successor, *The Guide for Biblical Studies.* Some sermons have been published by the *Christian Century Pulpit* and the *Pulpit Digest.*

While I am not a gifted poet, I have written a modest number of poems and have published a small booklet of Christmas verse. I have also written some hymns. The Anniversary Hymn for the Church of the Brethren's two hundred fiftieth anniversary celebration was my first published hymn. Four others have been published by the Hymn Society of America, and others have had limited use in church dedications, evangelism conferences, and Annual Conference.

Perhaps my most sustained ministry in the literary field has been my work with the journal, *Brethren Life and Thought*. At a day's retreat of the Bethany Seminary faculty and the Brotherhood staff in the fall of 1953, there were hours of good discussion about Brethren writing. The group was particularly challenged by Professor Donovan Smucker, who urged that the Brethren start a journal for the publication of scholarly work. The idea caught fire. At the Annual Conference of 1954, a group of interested people met and organized the Brethren Journal Association. During the ensuing year, an editorial board was appointed and a staff to start the journal. I considered it an honored trust when the Board asked me to be the editor. The journal was to be a quarterly, independent of any conference or General Board control. Out of my conversations with the editorial board, I formulated a statement of the plan and purposes of the journal, which I included in the first editorial. I wrote:

In the name of God, Amen! We present this first issue of *Brethren Life and Thought* conscious of a great cloud of witnesses and of the real and urgent need of the divine wisdom. This is a religious venture, launched in faith, dedicated to the quest for truth and to the highest interests of a church which is emerging as one of the lively and responsible members of the larger family, the Body of Christ. Therefore, we invoke the guidance of God and His blessing as we present this first number of our journal.

Brethren Life and Thought will carry on among Brethren and their friends a sustained, spirited, thoughtful conversation on the great issues we face today, and on our heritage. The Church of the Brethren has reached a position of considerable prestige, and of considerable danger. Which way will we go? What light can we find for the days of dangerous opportunity just ahead? Who are we and whence have we come? What is our role as a church in the larger family of the Christian Church? This journal offers itself as the medium of exchange for articles on all these issues, however controversial or urgent they may be. We will publish articles which deal with the whole range of Brethren thought, life, history, theology, culture, and philosophy.

We have no official ties, no subsidy. We believe we can serve the church we love in the best fashion if we do not seek any official sponsorship, either from our General Brotherhood Board, our conference, or our institutions of higher learning. We believe and pray that we will strengthen all of them by our ministry. We are not a competitor of the

Gospel Messenger, but seek to meet a need which a popular and universally read church organ cannot meet. We shall supplement each other's ministry. The Brethren Publishing House will print and mail the journal for the association, a relationship which the association and the staff appreciate and cherish. We are establishing the journal not out of a spirit of discontent or of criticism, but as an additional and greatly needed means of communication of sustained thought, scholarly research, and vigorous exchange of dedicated Brethren opinion.

O God, source of all wisdom, Fountain of all truth, Light of the minds that earnestly seek after Thee, Founder and Lord of the redemptive fellowship of the church, illuminate the pathway and accept the offering of our minds, hearts and hands in the journal here dedicated to Thy service. Make it an instrument of understanding, a channel of holy wisdom, a bond of Christian unity, a kindled torch of sharing love — that through its ministry, the church may be made stronger, the minds of Thy people made wiser, the Kingdom of our Lord Jesus Christ brought nearer in the hearts and minds of all men, through Jesus Christ our Lord, Amen.

When we began, our subscription price was three dollars per year. We hoped that many people would become members of the Brethren Journal Association, contributing ten dollars per year or more. As the years have passed, we have seen production costs go sky high. We never had many "angels" to bail us out. A few persons — Jack Kough, Clyde Carter, and Perry Rohrer among them — gave substantial amounts. The Brethren Press, who print and distribute the journal for us, have always been most cooperative, and patient when we were hard put to find funds for paying our bills. Several times the General Brotherhood Board gave a small subsidy, but always with seeming reluctance and a warning! We felt considerable resentment when the Board with apparent cheerfulness gave five thousand dollars to keep the *Christian Century* solvent, but expressed much concern when the journal needed one thousand dollars!

In recent years, Bethany Seminary has become a partner with the Brethren Journal Association in this venture. Some funds from a bequest from the estate of Dr. Perry Rohrer have cushioned our small deficits, and we are remaining almost solvent. All editorial work on the journal is volunteer service. We have not paid honoraria to writers, but have given each writer twenty off-prints of his article. Apparently there is enough prestige in having an article appear in our journal that authors are usually happy with this arrangement.

Our subscription list is not extensive. We have never had over a thousand subscribers, and the average per year would be near eight hundred. Many theological seminary libraries subscribe, and quite a number of college and local church libraries. As this book is getting its final revision we have completed the fall issue for 1979, thus completing Volume XXIV. I think the quality of materials we publish is better than ever. I never need to rush frantically about to find good materials. In recent years alternate issues are on special subjects or themes, and the others are a potpourri of general articles on a host of subjects. I am in the happy editorial position of having far more good articles come in than I can use!

Many persons have made the success of the journal possible. In our earlier years Frances Clemens (now Nyce) designed the cover and served as managing editor. Doris Cline Egge and later Alice G. Miller worked with me during some of the early years as assistant editors. My son, Donald Ziegler, designed the present cover. For the past several years, Ora Garber and later Mildred Heckert have given countless hours to making the journal as perfect a product as humanly possible. Ora was not only production editor for a number of years, but while book editor, he always went over the copy and proofs with unerring skill and loving care. He also provided excellent translations of many old German hymns of the Brethren, and frequent sensitive and finely crafted poems of his own. Since his retirement, Mildred Heckert has served with great skill and devotion as copy editor.

John A. Eichelberger has served through most of our publishing life as treasurer and business manager of the journal. As editor I have never needed to worry or bother about the business end of the project. It is superbly cared for!

Perhaps no other person has done as much to provide ideas, suggest writers, and actually write a number of excellent historical articles as Dr. Donald R. Durnbaugh, of the seminary faculty. He and Vernard Eller, whether or not they are on the editorial board, continue to be fountains of wisdom and inspiration for me.

I am happy to write that *BL&T* from time to time takes note of the lighter, frolicsome side of Brethren life! In an early issue we ran a delightful piece by C. Wayne Zunkel, on "The Posture of the Right Thumb During Opening Prayer in Morning Services During January in Leap Years!" Later we ran a few articles by "Pathfinder," a prominent young churchman who took some irreverent swipes at the church bureaucracy and leadership. We took some slaps on the editorial wrists for that! And we ran a series of good satires by Alexander Machiavelli, who also found plenty of grist for a court jester! One of our great achievements was the publication of a complete annotated bibliography of Brethren literature, in 1964. Groundwork for it had been done by the veteran educator, L. W. Shultz. It was completed and published by Donald Durnbaugh. Later a supplement was published. We hope to bring it back up to date in 1981.

This editorial task has been a most rewarding one, and I believe the journal has been a great benefit to the church. "The good Lord willing," and if senility does not overtake me, I hope to complete twenty-five years as editor of the journal. I have long urged the officers of the Brethren Journal Association to have someone in the bullpen to take over my duties when I falter or retire, and now they have done so. A perceptive scholar, Dr. Warren Kissinger, has begun service as associate editor.

CHAPTER 12

No Man Is An Island

*W*hat I have done, how I have lived, what I am today, I owe to a great many persons who have had powerful influences on my life. To list all would be a long and sparkling list indeed. But as I look back across the years, in addition to those nearest me, whose lives have been so deeply entwined with mine—my father and mother, Ilda who shared the totality of my life for forty-eight years, and in these latter years Mary Grace—I wish here to express my appreciation to a few who have helped to mould my life and thought.

I must first name my grandfather, *Jesse C. Ziegler*. His dignity, his wisdom as a church elder and a pioneer in education, his patience, and especially in my early teens when he suffered greatly and I was his gardener and coachman, his kindness to me; all these gave me my first ideal of ministry.

My uncle, *Samuel H. Ziegler,* stimulated my growth in countless ways. He gave me books which stretched my mind, got me started in my lifelong hobby of photography, took me on great hikes, and when I was drawn to the ministry, asked me sharp questions which made me probe deeply into motives.

Dr. Harold Miller, dedicated country physician and Christian philosopher, with his gracious wife, *Dr. Blanche Miller,* gave us counsel and encouragement when Ilda and I started our life together. He introduced me to the *Christian Century,* and demonstrated a rich combination of healing-teaching-counselling ministry. They were truly doctors of the whole person!

Dr. Paul Haynes Bowman, who was president of Bridgewater College when I came there as a student, was my ideal as a scholar, preacher, and perfect gentleman. He restored my vision, and opened doors for ministry for me. Because of his wise counsel and encouragement, I went on to my lifelong career as a minister. His quiet, eloquent sermons and his counsel put him very high on my list of elder friends.

During the early years of my ministry two men stand out as having enormous if somewhat more remote influence on me. One was *John R. Mott,* the great missionary statesman, founder of the Student Volunteer Movement, and architect of the ecumenical movement. His books and several series of lectures I heard him give gave me a strong world vision. The other was *Harry Emerson Fosdick,* the brilliant preacher who led the fight against fundamentalism in the 1920s. Like hundreds of other young preachers, I tried to emulate his preaching style, and was powerfully influenced by his sermons and his books. While I was in India, I used some of his books which had been translated into Gujarati. Once I ordered a new book of his sermons. The day it arrived, Ilda was seriously ill, and I had gone through a crisis in my work. I opened the book and found his sermon on "The High Uses of Trouble." It spoke to my deepest need. I read it, then read it aloud to Ilda. It gave us great comfort and courage. I immediately wrote him a letter of appreciation for the spiritual lift we had received. I had no expectation of a reply, but by return mail I had a beautiful hand-written letter from him which was so gracious and warm-hearted that I ever after counted him a most helpful friend!

A truly great teacher in Bridgewater College was the saintly scholar, *John S. Flory.* From him I learned the beauty of real literature, in the Old Testament, and in the great English poets. Dr. Flory was then an old man, but he lived on to be a gracious supporter of my ministry when I became his pastor, twenty years later!

Perhaps no leader in the Church of the Brethren was more greatly loved than *Charles D. Bonsack.* As foreign mission secretary, he was the person who encouraged us to go to India. He wrote long and wise letters to all missionaries, and was a most gracious interpreter of the mission to the home church. He made each one of us feel important, and could give the most astute guidance when we needed it, the most kindly comfort and encouragement when we needed that. He was a missionary statesman and a "father in God."

John H. Reisner, once dean of the college of agriculture in Nanking, China, was the first executive of Agricultural Missions, Inc. and the Christian Rural Fellowship. It was he who found my first book on worship, and published and promoted it widely. He was not an eloquent speaker, but a man of great vision and executive ability. He gave me great encouragement to explore, write, and teach in the field of worship among the rural churches. And it was he who encouraged me to write other books and appointed me consultant on Rural Worship to Agricultural Missions, Inc.

148

Even before arriving in India, I had been greatly influenced by the famous evangelist, *E. Stanley Jones.* He was a popular Methodist preacher who was able to draw great crowds of people, especially the educated classes, to his preaching all over India. While our paths crossed infrequently, we were able to have Dr. Jones in a week's preaching mission in Surat. Seven hundred to a thousand people came every night to hear him. To some extent I patterned my own missionary approach after his, and had I returned to India, I would have carried this type of ministry much further, especially in Gujarat. His books, too, have done much to mold my thought.

While in India, I heard the famous Japanese Christian leader, *Toyokiko Kagawa.* He was an evangelist, a poet, and a great Christian social reformer. A most Christlike figure, Kagawa suffered greatly. His ministry, unhappily, was eclipsed by the tragedy of World War II.

In the years since returning from India — the longer part of my career — persons who have most influenced my thought and ministry have been *Rufus D. Bowman,* who was president of Bethany Theological Seminary from 1937 to 1952 when he died at the height of his career; *William Beahm,* who taught me to love and do theology; *Ira Moomaw,* who was a great colleague in India, then became secretary of Agricultural Missions, Inc., and one of the world's leading authorities on hunger and the Christian response to it.

Writers who have most greatly stimulated my thought have been the Quaker philosopher, *D. Elton Trueblood;* the South African scholar and novelist, *Alan Paton; Dr. Paul Tournier,* the Swiss physician of the whole person; *Robert Frost,* salty New England poet; and *C. S. Lewis,* British scholar and author.

Virginia Showalter Fisher, one of the most learned of Christian educators in the Church of the Brethren, has for many years been an inspiration and a challenge to me, and was a great friend and colleague to Ilda in children's work. Virginia is a writer, has been guest editor of *Brethren Life and Thought,* and still eggs me on to write. She could have been a fine moderator for a Brethren Annual Conference! Her husband, *Nevin,* too, has been a great friend and encourager. He is a fine combination of concert pianist, teacher and philosopher!

Perhaps no one in the past several years of my life has been closer in spirit, or more of an encourager of my ministry, than my brother-in-law, *Desmond W. Bittinger,* and his wife, *Irene.* His gracious and humble spirit, his superb skills as teacher, preacher, and writer, his ecumenical spirit, the depth of his faith, have endeared him to many thousands of people, and have made him not only a relative but a warm friend and true brother in Christ to me.

CHAPTER 13

Credo

Some years ago, The *Christian Century* published a series of articles by distinguished thinkers under the general title of "How My Mind Has Changed." Some of these leaders were able to chart a course of theological maturing and centering down on eternal verities. For others, it seemed that they had lost their moorings and were still adrift in a stormy sea of conflict without chart or compass.

It seems to me that as I sum up the years of my pilgrimage, I should look back over my course and see what the development of my own life has been. Perhaps a brief statement of my present credo also can help me at least to clarify the meanderings of my mind or at best the progress of my thought about life and the beacon lights which have lured me on.

There was nothing complex or shadowy about my boyhood faith. It was formed by the simple piety of my mother, and the strong biblical faith and puritan ethic of my father. The teaching and preaching I heard were not theologically oriented but rather a simple, forthright proclaiming of orthodox Christian faith and morals. About the only strong leaning I can perceive in my early faith was a deep interest in the idea of creation, and a perception that the earth with all its creatures was the Lord's; that we could know much about God through understanding His works in the universe. I recall that at the time I was ordained, I went through a period of questioning and did not know where to turn for certainties.

Then I was exposed to the powerful currents of premillennialist fundamentalism. Quite a few ministers in the Church of the Brethren, especially W. K. Conner, who spent weeks preaching in our church, were completely immersed in this trend. I associated with an interdenominational group of laymen who met regularly for Bible study, using the Scofield Bible as the only true and perfect framework of the Holy Word. Yet, I found myself drawing away from this theology, as did my father also. We talked much, and sought for more light. The teaching of E. B. Hoff in three weeks at Elizabethtown College, and the influence of teachers like Ezra Wenger and Franklin J. Byer, helped me to grope toward more light.

The greatest impetus toward a more steady and sound biblical faith came through long talks with Dr. Harold Miller, and then my courses in Bible at Bridgewater College. Drs. Paul Bowman and Frederick Dove were trained at Crozer Theological Seminary, and Minor C. Miller at Boston University. They were liberal in their thought, yet were good biblical scholars. Through their influence, and that of Harry Emerson Fosdick and such ecumenical leaders as John R. Mott and Sherwood Eddy, I moved completely away from fundamentalism, and toward a biblical liberalism. My ideas of the Bible were largely formed by such books as Fosdick's *Guide to Understanding the Bible,* with its eloquent exposition of progressive revelation, and Julius Bewer's *The Literature of the Old Testament.*

During my years in India, I could only share the Gospel as I was able to see it in living confrontation with the religions of India. I came to see it as the fulfillment of the highest promise of Hinduism, Islam and Buddhism; Christian faith is *The Crown of Hinduism,* as J. N. Farquhar so well put it in the profound book by that name. My work there made me constantly reexamine my faith. *A Layman's Inquiry Into Foreign Missions,* which was a severe critique of the whole basis and program of missions, was helpful in turning the spotlight on some assumptions which we could not sustain. Later, the profound study by Dr. Hendrik Kraemer entitled, *The Christian Message in a Non-Christian World,* which made us turn again to see the discontinuity between the Gospel and the religious quests of mankind, had a salutary effect, and clarified for us the sharp challenge of the Gospel to all religious systems. These years were a time of challenge and ferment. The experiences and challenges helped greatly in clarifying and stabilizing my own faith and the message I had to share.

I had come to a great appreciation of the rich spiritual heritage of India, expressed in all the living religions rooted there. I saw that the Gospel of Christ was a true fulfillment and a fresh new wind of hope and light, of promise and power for India. I saw, too, that the water of life which Jesus Christ came to offer, must be given to India not in Western forms but in an Indian cup. There is a solid core of ultimate truth in the Gospel, absolutely essential to human life everywhere. But it must be proclaimed in the language of the people. The Christ we offered must wear Indian dress and walk the Indian road. Only so would He be welcomed, heard, followed and obeyed. It was my firm belief that, great as Mahatma Gandhi was and however brilliantly he demonstrated much of the Sermon on the Mount, he, too, —even he—needed Jesus Christ not only as mentor, but as Savior and Lord.

My views on the Bible, while I do not say they have come full circle, have matured into a profound belief in the authority of the Bible as the Word of God. I believe Jesus Christ is the ultimate, perfect Word of God, the Logos. He comes to me through the Bible. God's unfolding purpose is revealed in both Old and New Testaments, and comes to full and complete revelation in Him. I have no difficulty accepting the facts of the multiple documentary sources of the Bible. I believe that in a very real sense God inspired the writers to convey the revelation He vouchsafed to them. I cannot accept the usual concept of literal inerrancy. I do not think the Bible is intended to give an inerrant account of science and history, or that its chronology is infallible. I am certain that many times when the Bible accounts declare, "God commanded us to do this," ancient peoples were stating what they understood God to say. But only in Christ do we at last have the perfect revelation of His will and purpose.

I regard the Bible as a totally trustworthy guide to faith and life. I read the total Bible in the light of the truth of God revealed in the life, death, teaching, and resurrection of Jesus Christ the Lord. And I find that the writers of the New Testament, especially of the epistles, were and are faithful interpreters of Christ and the Kingdom of love and grace He established. I am not a fundamentalist, nor a literalist. But I believe I am an orthodox, evangelical disciple of Jesus Christ, commissioned to be a servant of the Word. I find that my views of Christ and of God and His purposes have possibly been most clearly illuminated and clarified by the profound teaching of Karl Barth. With some slight reservations here and there, I would classify myself as neo-orthodox!

For many years I would have called myself a pacifist. I believe that the classical form of political pacificism which seems to be nearer to Gandhi's non-violent resistance than to the way of the Cross of Jesus, is not the perfect model of discipleship. I have long cherished the term which I believe was coined by Dr. Paul Bowman, *creative peace-making*. I am drawn strongly to the stance of radical discipleship, which often sets the disciple in opposition to the claims of the state. I must obey God rather than men; my allegiance where there is conflict, is to God rather than to Caesar. At the same time I am slow to trust solely to my private judgment as to what belongs to God and what to Caesar. I believe in being a good citizen, in voting, in seeking in Christian ways to influence legislation and world affairs. At the same time, all of my acts as a citizen of the state must be seen in the white light of my prior obligation as a citizen of the Kingdom of God.

Some years ago, I found myself caught up, though with some qualms, in the idea that the church must let the world set its agenda, that a servant church is almost a servant social agency of the world. I have deep concerns at this point now. I believe the church must first hear what God is saying, in mercy and compassion *and in judgment.* It is God, who knows the world's needs better than we can, who hears the cries of his people in bondage, who calls us and sets the agenda, not the strident, demanding, conflicting voices of the world. As Jesus was the "man for others," so must the church be the "community of faith for others." The church has its charter in Jesus' own mission to bring God's *Shalom* to the world, and His clear and insistent call, "as the Father sent me, so send I you." I believe more strongly than ever that the church's mission is evangelism, in the highest, noblest sense of the word. While long ago I may have thought of evangelism as calling people to get ready for Heaven, I think of it now, as D. T. Niles so well has said, "as one hungry beggar telling another where he has found bread."

The rise in recent years of a strong and rather widely spread neo-Pentecostal movement in the Church of the Brethren has given me much concern. On the one hand, the renewed emphasis upon the power and pre-eminence of the Holy Spirit in the life of the church has been salutary. On the other hand, the insistent claim that all persons who receive "the baptism in the Holy Spirit" must and actually do speak in tongues of ecstasy has been divisive and is scripturally wrong. Often the freshness and joy which characterize those who have had this experience are diluted by a retreat to a narrow fundamentalism. I am particularly disturbed by the claim that only those who have experienced the stylized and rather rigid forms of this baptism in the Spirit are charismatic. As I understand the scriptures there are many spiritual gifts, and all of us who rejoice in our use of these gifts and are growing in the spiritual graces which Paul describes in Galatians 5:22 are truly charismatic.

Therefore I rejoice in the renewed emphasis upon the Holy Spirit, and in the joy and freedom which many have found in this movement. At the same time I would insist that far more of us are truly charismatic, though not Pentecostal. There needs to be much greater acceptance of one another. The Holy Spirit is never divisive. When the neo-Pentecostal experience divides, surely the Holy Spirit is not in it! I thank God for the great winds of the Holy Spirit which I feel are moving our beloved church, and I am glad they are far too powerful for me or any other person to direct!

I am concerned that my beloved church has sometimes spent the greater part of its energies and resources in ministering only to the material part of humanity's needs. I would not have us in any way decrease our concern for food and human rights, for dignity and justice. But I would have us maintain a holistic approach, meeting the whole needs of persons. We must never divorce service and evangelism, nor water down our proclamation of the Gospel by assuming that our brothers and sisters are so low that bread and votes and absence of war will be sufficient to meet all their need. The mission of the church as I now see it is to share the Good News of God through kerygma—the proclamation; diakonia —serving; and koinonia—the loving community. Only then shall God's whole will be done!

INDEX

Date Due

BRODART, INC. Cat. No. 23 233 Printed in U.S